CW00328251

REVISE AQA GCSE (9–1)
History
NORMAN ENGLAND, c1066–c1100

REVISION
GUIDE AND WORKBOOK

Series Consultant: Harry Smith

Author: Sally Clifford

Also available to support your revision:

Revise GCSE Study Skills Guide   9781447967071

The **Revise GCSE Study Skills Guide** is full of tried-and-trusted hints and tips for how to learn more effectively. It gives you techniques to help you achieve your best – throughout your GCSE studies and beyond!

Revise GCSE Revision Planner   9781447967828

The **Revise GCSE Revision Planner** helps you to plan and organise your time, step-by-step, throughout your GCSE revision. Use this book and wall chart to mastermind your revision.

> **For the full range of Pearson revision titles across KS2, KS3, GCSE, Functional Skills, AS/A Level and BTEC visit:**
> www.pearsonschools.co.uk/revise

Contents

. . . .

A small bit of small print

AQA publishes Sample Assessment Material and the Specification on its website. This is the official content and this book should be used in conjunction with it. The questions and revision tasks in this book have been written to help you revise the skills you may need for your assessment. Remember: the real assessment may not look like this.

Anglo-Saxon England

In order to understand the impact of the Norman Conquest, you need to know what England was like before 1066.

Kings of England from 871

Timeline

871–899 Alfred the Great, King of Wessex: fought the Danes and established the dynasty that would unite England.

899–978 The rule of the direct descendants of Alfred the Great.

978–1016 Æthelred the Unready: great, great grandson of Alfred the Great, deposed by Cnut, King of Denmark (a Viking). Æthelred's elder son, Edmund Ironside, keeps Wessex until his death, then Cnut rules the whole of England.

1016–1035 Cnut

1035–1040 Harold Harefoot, elder son of Cnut

1040–1042 Harthacnut, second son of Cnut

1042 Edward the Confessor, Æthelred's younger son, takes the throne.

Although Alfred the Great fought the Danes and began the unification of England, parts of the north of England remained under Danish control – this area was called the 'Danelaw'.

Society in Anglo-Saxon England

There were just six earldoms, which meant that the earls were very powerful. Together with the leading bishops, the earls formed the **Witan** – the king's advisors. The Witan was very influential, but the king did not have to take their advice.

The king owned more land than anyone else, and controlled the courts. The king could also raise taxes and issue laws. The people relied on the strength of the king.

There were about 4000 **thegns**. They ran the local courts and collected taxes, and were expected to fight for the king if necessary.

Most people in England were peasant farmers. Ceorls were free peasants – some owned their own land, others paid rent to a thegn and often had to work for him for 2–3 days a week.

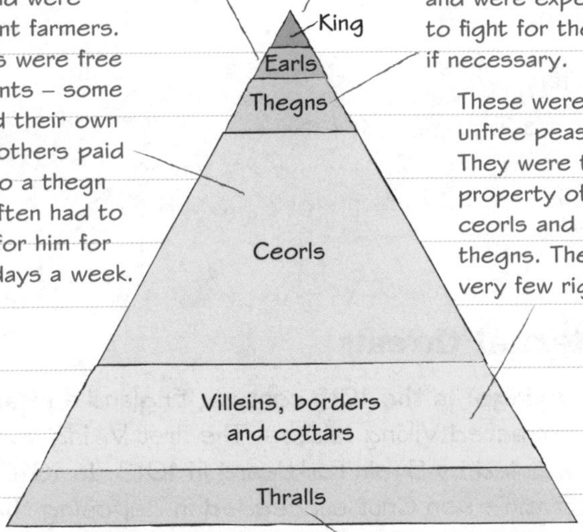
King
Earls
Thegns
Ceorls
Villeins, borders and cottars
Thralls

These were unfree peasants. They were the property of the ceorls and the thegns. They had very few rights.

These were slaves and made up about 10 per cent of the population.

Anglo-Saxon England was a wealthy country. See page 2 for more.

The Church

The influence of Irish missionaries, such as St Patrick (385–461), meant that the English Church developed its own identity, unique from the church in the rest of Europe.

In the 10th century, England had a thriving Church – mainly due to the work of St Dunstan, who was Archbishop of Canterbury from 960 to 978. Dunstan reformed the Church and improved the standard of the clergy.

After Dunstan's death, standards declined due to Viking raids that destroyed most of Canterbury. Cnut and his sons were Christian, and supported the Church, but it never recovered the strength it had under Dunstan.

Culture

Anglo-Saxon England had a flourishing culture.

- There were skilled craftsmen producing high quality art, especially engravings, enamel and metalwork.
- A variety of literature, poems, histories and stories were written, and maps were drawn.
- The most famous Anglo-Saxon work of fiction is *Beowulf*, a story that continues to be read today, and new versions are still published.

The Alfred Jewel is the finest example of Anglo-Saxon art. It features high-quality enamel and intricate metalwork in gold.

Now try this

Some historians describe Anglo-Saxon England as a 'golden age'. Why do you think this is?

The succession crisis, 1066

When King Edward the Confessor died in 1066, it was unclear who should have the throne. This was because England's complicated history led to multiple claimants.

England in 1065

By 1065, England had existed as a single country for just over a hundred years. Before that, it had been divided into regions, each with its own ruler.

King Edward the Confessor ruled England between 1042 and 1066. He was a very religious man, but a weak king. He left the running of the kingdom to his advisors (the Witan) while he focused his energies on the Church.

> You won't be asked any questions about the period before 1066 in the exam, but it is still important – you won't be able to understand the events of 1066 without it.

Wealth and trade

England's fertile farmland meant that the economy was based on agriculture. Farmers produced wheat, rye, barley and oats, as well as animal products such as meat, cheese and leather.

Natural resources like timber, iron, lead and copper were another important source of wealth.

During the Anglo-Saxon period, England became an important trading nation, exporting food, raw materials and leather goods. However, the most important trade was the **wool trade** – English woollen cloth was highly valued in Europe.

> The earls were the most important men in the country after the king. They governed large areas on the king's behalf: collecting taxes, running the courts and raising the king's army.

External threats

1 **Vikings:** In the 10th century, England's wealth attracted Viking raiders. The first Viking invasion was led by Svein Forkbeard in 1013. In 1016, Svein's son Cnut succeeded in deposing the English king Æthelred – the father of Edward the Confessor. Cnut and then his sons went on to rule England for 26 years. Although the Vikings lost control of England in 1042, they still saw the kingdom as a valuable prize.

2 **Normans:** After the death of his father, Edward the Confessor was raised in the Norman court by his uncle, the Duke of Normandy. When he became King of England after the death of Harthacnut, Edward kept good relations with the Norman rulers. These connections led to the threat from Normandy.

Internal threats: the Godwins

> The most powerful family in England was the Godwins, the Earls of Wessex. They were always looking to expand their influence.

⬇

> In 1051, the Godwins rebelled against Edward. The earls of Northumbria and Mercia supported Edward and the Godwins were exiled. Edward appointed Norman advisers, as he felt he could trust them.

⬇

> The Witan resented Edward turning to the Normans for advice and encouraged the Godwins to return to England, which they did. The Godwin family regained their power, and Edward made Harold Godwinson **sub-regulus** (effectively his deputy).

Why was England such a prize?

The English throne was attractive because:

- ✓ it was wealthy – it had valuable resources and booming trade
- ✓ its kings had much stronger central control than other European rulers, thanks to an efficient administration
- ✓ its efficient administration made it easy to collect taxes, thereby increasing the king's wealth.

> Remember: the Normans, the Vikings and the Earls of Wessex had all wanted the English throne for years. When Edward died without a clear heir, they all saw their chance.

Now try this

Pick **one** thing that made England attractive to would-be invaders, and **one** thing that did not. Write a sentence for each explaining why you think this is.

The claimants to the throne

Choosing a king

In 11th century England, when a king died, it was not always straightforward to decide who would be the next king, especially if the dead king had no children.

Who became king was often a matter of luck, force and alliances because there was no set pattern. Ideally, they would be:

- ✓ a direct relative of the previous king
- ✓ chosen by the previous king
- ✓ supported by the Witan
- ✓ an experienced warrior
- ✓ wealthy and powerful enough to protect England from attack.

Promises and last words

In England, a king's last words before he died overruled any promises he might have made in the past. Harold Godwinson claimed that Edward the Confessor had promised him the throne just before he died.

In Normandy, a promise of the throne was final, and could not be undone – even on the king's deathbed. William of Normandy claimed that Edward had promised him the throne in 1051 – in return for helping him against the Godwins.

Edward the Confessor as depicted on the Bayeux Tapestry.

You can find out more about the Godwin family on page 2.

The four claimants to the throne in 1066

	Edgar Ætheling (c1051–c1126)	Harold Godwinson (c1022–66)	Harald Hardrada (c1015–66)	William of Normandy (c1028–87)
Direct relative of King Edward?	Yes As Edward's great nephew, he was the closest male relative	No But he had acted as Edward's sub regulus	No But King Harthacnut had promised the throne to Hardrada's father – Hardrada believed that he had inherited this claim	No Although William was a distant cousin of Edward's
Chosen by King Edward?	No	He claimed Edward chose him on his deathbed	No	He claimed Edward promised him the throne in 1051
Chosen by the Witan?	Rejected	Accepted	Ignored	Ignored
A strong warrior?	No	Yes	Yes	Yes
Wealthy and powerful?	No	Yes	Yes	Yes

Harold's oath

The Normans claimed that Harold had sworn an oath promising to support William's claim to the throne. The pope supported William's claim and gave him the **Papal Banner** (a banner that William could carry to show that he had God's blessing).

The English claimed that Harold had sworn the oath while being held prisoner and being threatened, so he could not be held to it.

Harold is crowned king

Whatever the strengths of the rival claims, Harold had the immediate advantage, and he took it – he was crowned King of England on 6 January 1066: the day after the death of Edward the Confessor.

Harold knew that he would be challenged – this was why he was crowned so quickly.

Now try this

Using the information on this page, write a short paragraph explaining whether you think William or Harold had the stronger claim, and why.

Preparing for battle

When William heard about Harold's coronation in 1066, he was furious. He sent a message to Harold, asking him to honour his oath. Harold ignored this – but knew that an invasion was coming.

Harold prepares for battle

1 First, Harold assembled a **navy**. As he had only just become king, he did not have any ships of his own, so he called up ships and sailors from all over the country. He very soon had a large navy.

2 Next he gathered his **army**. Anglo-Saxon kings did not have their own army – they had a small band of professional soldiers (the **housecarls**). However, in times of war, the king called on the **thegns** (lords) to fight for him. The thegns would bring ordinary men with them – they formed the **fyrd**.

> The housecarls were well-trained and well-armed.

> The fyrd were inexperienced fighters, and ill-equipped, but they fought with whatever weapons they could find and could be very effective.

By May, Harold had his navy – and several thousand troops – waiting on the south coast for William to invade. Edwin and Morcar, earls loyal to Harold, were guarding the north of England.

William prepares to invade

> Before William could begin to prepare for invasion, he had to win over some of his countrymen, who thought invading England was too risky. Getting the pope's support, and promising land in England if he won, eventually persuaded his fellow Normans to support him.

> Like Harold, William had no army of his own, and had to persuade his **vassals** (men who had sworn allegiance to him) to provide soldiers. Assembling his invasion force took time, but eventually William had 7000 soldiers, including **archers** and **cavalry**.

> To move the soldiers across the Channel, William needed ships. He ordered hundreds of ships to be built – this was a slow process, delaying the invasion.

> William also knew that he would need to secure his men once he got to England. The Normans built wooden castles to control the land and keep troops safe. William built **pre-fabricated castles** to take with him to England, meaning pre-made sections could be quickly assembled.

Norman ships as portrayed in the Bayeux Tapestry.

Harold's problem

While William was assembling his army, building ships and pre-fabricating castles, Harold spent three months waiting on the south coast. On 8 September 1066, Harold disbanded his army because:

👎 his soldiers wanted paying

👎 they were hungry

👎 he was running out of resources

👎 the fyrd were needed at home to bring in the harvest.

> Harold may have assumed that William's men were also needed for the harvest, and that it was safe to let his army disband.

Now try this

Give **three** reasons why William's preparations took longer than Harold's. Write a sentence for each reason, explaining why it was important.

The Battle of Stamford Bridge

A few days after Harold disbanded his army in September 1066, he heard that Harald Hardrada had invaded and captured the city of York.

Tostig

Harold's brother Tostig had been Earl of Northumbria but had lost his position and been sent into exile. Angry, Tostig went to Harald Hardrada to persuade him to invade England.

Tostig wasn't loyal to the Vikings – he was just looking for an opportunity to regain his own position.

The Battle of Fulford

Hardrada and Tostig's fleet of 300 ships landed at Riccall, near York, and then their soldiers marched towards the city on 20 September 1066.

Earls Edwin and Morcar tried to defend the city but were defeated – although they escaped with their lives. The city of York surrendered to Hardrada.

The Battle of Stamford Bridge

After hearing of Hardrada's arrival, Harold regathers his army and marches north – travelling nearly 200 miles in under a week.

⬇

More troops join Harold on his way north.

⬇

Harold expects to have to attack York, but finds Hardrada, Tostig and their army have left. He marches his army straight through the city.

⬇

Hardrada and Tostig are caught by surprise at Stamford Bridge on 25 September 1066 – the Vikings are not even wearing their **chain-mail**.

⬇

The fighting lasts all day – thousands of men are killed, including Hardrada and Tostig. Eventually the English break the Viking shield wall, and the Vikings surrender.

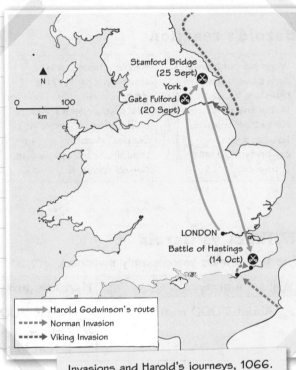

Invasions and Harold's journeys, 1066.

The flowchart demonstrates how even though Stamford Bridge was a victory for Harold, the impact overall was mainly negative.

How successful was Stamford Bridge?

Stamford Bridge was a great victory because ...

It was good for morale.

England was safe from Viking invasion.

However ...

It may have made Harold complacent.

England was unprotected against the Normans.

Having to move north and back would have tired Harold's troops.

The many dead and wounded were losses Harold could not afford.

Now try this

Identify **two** reasons why Harold won at Stamford Bridge. Write a sentence explaining each point.

Before the Battle of Hastings

While Harold was occupied fighting Tostig and Hardrada, William prepared to invade England.

For more about William's preparations, go to page 4.

The Normans land in England

The Norman invasion of England was delayed by bad weather. The wind turned in William's favour towards the end of September.

The Norman fleet landed at Pevensey on the Sussex coast on 28 September and William chose it as his base to raid the local area. Harold was still in the north.

Pevensey was a good choice of landing point. There was an old Roman fort, protected by a bay. The Normans built their first castle inside the old fort. Remains of the castle exist today.

Harold's reaction

When Harold heard about the Norman invasion, he was still in the north. He set off towards London again, covering 200 miles in a week.	Harold's housecarls travelled with him. He gathered an army in London, and gave orders for more soldiers to assemble in Sussex. Harold's advisors thought he should wait, but Harold refused.	It was clear that neither William nor Harold was going to give up the English throne without a fight.	Harold arrived near Hastings on 13 October. Despite Harold's hasty arrival, William knew that he was coming and at dawn on 14 October, the Normans marched out to meet Harold's army, who were camped near Senlac Hill.

Some historians think Harold was angry about William's **plundering** of the south coast. Others suggest that he was hoping to surprise William as he had surprised Hardrada, although it appears they did exchange messages before the battle.

William vs Harold

The two armies were evenly matched.

William's army	Harold's army
👍 About 7000 men	👍 About 7000 men
	👎 Others were trying to join him but were still a long way away. If Harold had waited, he might have had 14000 men.
👍 The Norman soldiers were well rested.	👎 Many of the men who had fought at Stamford Bridge were tired or wounded.
👎 William's troops stood at the bottom of the hill.	👍 Harold chose a ridge near Hastings, with a forest behind it – this gave him a strong defensive line.
	👎 The forest would make retreat difficult.
👍 William's army consisted of knights on horseback, archers and infantry.	👎 Harold had no horsemen or archers.
	👍 His foot soldiers formed a deep line, protected by a wall of shields.
👍 The Normans fought with swords and wore chain-mail.	👍 The thegns fought with swords and javelins.
	👍 The fyrd carried weapons like axes, clubs, scythes and pitchforks. These were simple weapons, but very effective.

Now try this

Write a paragraph explaining the advantages and disadvantages of Harold's decision to attack William at once.

The Battle of Hastings

The Anglo-Saxon and Norman armies were the same size, but there were important differences between them. Both had advantages and disadvantages that affected the outcome of the battle.

Key terms

- ✓ **Housecarls** – trained soldiers who were also bodyguards to their lord.
- ✓ **Fyrd** – working men, mainly peasants, who were called to fight for the king in times of war. This allowed the army to be replenished after each battle.
- ✓ **Shield wall** – making a defensive 'wall' with shields, to protect the army's line. Bands within the fyrd would have known each other well, making the shield wall more effective.
- ✓ **Feigned retreat** – pretending to retreat to tempt the enemy to follow so that they could be surrounded and killed. This was a well-known Norman tactic.
- ✓ **Mercenaries** – soldiers who fought for whoever would pay them.

Norman knights vs English housecarls

Norman knights:

- 👍 They were highly trained, heavily armoured and rode horses. They could launch devastating charges using their height to beat down foes.
- 👎 Horses were vulnerable to attack.
- 👎 The advantages of a cavalry charge were lost if horses had to run uphill.

English housecarls:

- 👍 A disciplined **shield wall** was very hard to break. Housecarls knew how to fight together and their axes were highly effective.
- 👎 Housecarls were vulnerable to cavalry and archer attacks if the shield wall broke.

Norman foot soldiers vs English fyrd

William's foot soldiers were a mixture of Normans and mercenaries from across Europe. There were lightly armoured archers and crossbowmen and heavily armoured foot soldiers. Foot soldiers may not have trained with knights, making coordinated attacks difficult.

The thegns were well-armed with swords and javelins, but the fyrd fought with whatever weapons they had – clubs, axes, scythes and pitchforks. Harold had no archers.

The Battle of Hastings

Harold's army was able to position itself along a ridge at the top of a hill. That meant that William had to attack uphill.

⬇

The battle lasted eight hours – a very long time for a medieval battle. This was perhaps because the two sides were quite evenly matched. There were different phases to the battle.

⬇

William's archers were first to attack, but the archers had to stay out of English javelin range and the English shield wall knew how to catch the arrows on their shields.

⬇

William's foot soldiers and knights were beaten back by the shield wall initially. The English **housecarls** did great damage to horses and men with their two-handed axes.

⬇

At one point the Norman army was panicking that William had been killed. William tipped back his helmet to show he was still alive.

⬇

The turning point was when the Normans retreated. The English broke ranks to chase them, weakening their line. The Normans were probably carrying out a tactic called a **feigned retreat**.

⬇

The shield wall was gradually thinned out. Norman knights then charged through it and caused great damage. Norman archers also became more effective as the shield wall failed.

⬇

Harold and his brothers, Gyrth and Leofwine, and their housecarls, made final stands at the top of the hill, fighting to the death. Harold and his brothers were killed.

⬇

With Harold dead, the rest of the English army began to flee.

Now try this

Describe **one** advantage and **one** disadvantage of the Norman foot soldiers and **one** advantage and **one** disadvantage of the English fyrd troops.

Reasons for William's victory

Harold was ultimately defeated at the Battle of Hastings. Both armies had strengths and skills but the Normans were able to take advantage of Harold's mistakes and William's luck.

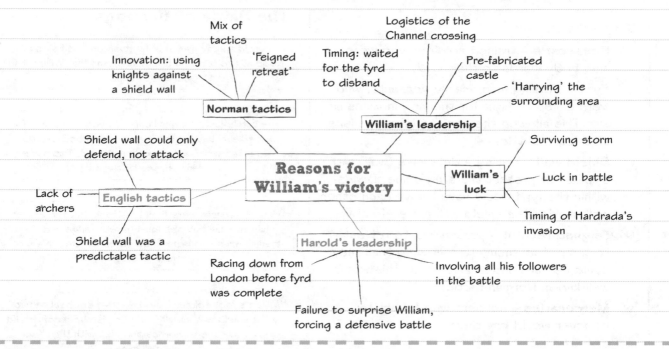

Battle advantages

Harold	William of Normandy
👍 Harold was fighting on home ground: Wessex. 👍 The housecarls were experienced, disciplined and skilled warriors. 👍 The English had the best position on the battlefield: on a ridge at the top of the hill.	👍 William's troops were trained in tactics that the English had never experienced before, including the feigned retreat. 👍 His troops had to fight to survive: they would not be able to retreat or escape. 👍 William had obtained the pope's blessing for his invasion and he and his men believed that God was on their side.

Battle disadvantages

Harold	William of Normandy
👎 The men of the general fyrd were inexperienced and lacked discipline. 👎 The core of his army was tired from fighting at Stamford Bridge and marching south. They may also have been demoralised by having to fight yet another battle. 👎 Harold did not have any archers.	👎 Having to fight uphill made knights and archers less effective. 👎 Although his knights had trained for years in their battle tactics, many of his foot soldiers were mercenaries who had not trained to fight in combination with knights. 👎 Knights had trained to charge against other knights: charging a shield wall was probably something entirely new.

Now try this

What do you think was the most important factor in William's victory? Write a sentence explaining your choice.

William establishes control

William had won the Battle of Hastings but this did not make him king immediately. Before he could be crowned, he had to take control of the kingdom.

William secures the south

⑥ William was crowned King of England at Westminster Abbey on Christmas Day, 1066. The atmosphere was tense and fighting broke out outside the Abbey.

④ He took the royal **treasury** (where the royal wealth was kept) at Winchester.

① After the Battle of Hastings, William hoped that the English would surrender. However, the Witan chose to make Edgar Ætheling king.

⑤ He then headed to London, setting up camp outside the city at Barking. Meanwhile, many nobles became concerned about Edgar's ability to rule. In December, Edgar came to William to surrender the kingdom.

③ He then marched through Kent, looting, terrorising the population and building castles as he went, before taking Canterbury.

② William took Dover, securing the route back to the coast.

Berkhamsted · London · Barking · Canterbury · Wallingford · Winchester · Dover · Pevensey · Hastings

The march on London

From Hastings to Dover

William's march on London.

Dealing with the English nobles

William wanted to show that he was the legitimate (entitled) ruler of England, so he tried to make sure there was continuity between Edward the Confessor's reign and his own.

William took control ...

| But he also ... |

Claiming all English land and giving the land of those who died at Hastings to his supporters. ⟹ Allowed English earls and thegns who had not fought at Hastings to buy back their land.

Putting his closest allies in charge of the south. ⟹ Allowed English nobles to keep their positions if they submitted to him.

Taking Edgar Ætheling, Edwin and Morcar with him to Normandy to discourage rebellion. ⟹ Kept them in comfort rather than having them imprisoned or killed.

Controlling the borderlands

William created three new earldoms (Hereford, Shrewsbury and Chester) to protect the Marches – the border with Wales. The Marcher earls had special rights and privileges. They:

☑ could create new towns to promote Norman colonisation of the Marches

☑ had total control: their sheriffs reported to them not to the king

☑ did not have to pay tax on their lands, so they could invest in defence

☑ could build castles as they wished.

Hugh d'Avranches, William FitzOsbern and Roger de Montgomery were followers of William and had supported him in the invasion. They became the first three Marcher earls.

Securing the throne

In March 1067, William returned to Normandy. To secure his throne while he was away, he took several precautions.

As well as appointing the Marcher earls, William put William FitzOsbern, his closest friend, in charge of East Anglia, and his half-brother, Odo of Bayeux, in control of the south east, both vulnerable areas.

How William attempted to secure his throne

William instructed his nobles to build castles on their land to subdue the local people.

William took key English nobles with him to Normandy (see above).

William's precautions were not enough to prevent rebellion, and he soon had to return.

See page 11 for more on the rebellions.

Now try this

Give **three** examples of ways in which William established control over England.

Castles

Everywhere the Normans went, they built castles – they were absolutely vital to William's control of England.

Norman castles

A palisade (strong fence) was made of solid timbers driven deep into the ground: it was strong and quick to build. Sometimes a double fence with earth packed in between was built.

Access to the tower was either up steep steps cut into the motte or, in some castles, up a sort of bridge.

A strong wooden tower, sometimes called the keep, provided a lookout point, an elevated attack position for archers to defend the whole area of the castle and a final point of defence from attack.

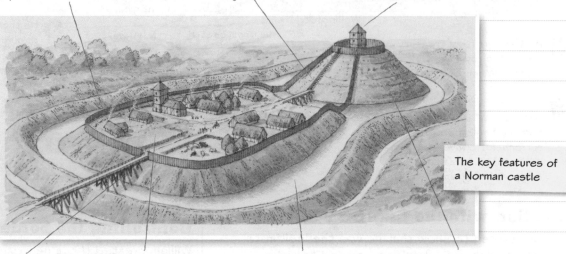

The key features of a Norman castle

Access into the castle was controlled through the gatehouse. Sometimes a drawbridge over the ditch could be pulled up to defend the gatehouse from attack.

The bailey was the enclosure below the motte and also protected by the palisade and outer defences, where the stables and barracks would be for the garrison of troops. During attacks, local people and livestock could take shelter here.

A ditch was cut that surrounded both the bailey and the motte. Sometimes the ditch was filled with water, protecting the palisade.

The motte was a large mound of earth, typically 5–7 metres high. Because it was earth, it was fireproof. With enough peasant labour a motte was quick to build. Most motte and bailey castles took between four and nine months to construct.

- -

They were used to **garrison** soldiers who could suppress or deter rebellion. A network of castles meant troops could be moved to where they were most needed.

The tower was used as a lookout point, keeping the local population under surveillance.

Castles reminded the English who was in control. They were dominating structures that overlooked the surrounding area. They would have had a huge psychological impact.

The Normans often destroyed houses and workshops to make space for their castles.

Strategy

Why and where the Normans built castles: short-term reasons

Symbolism

They were built in **strategically** important places, for example, to ensure that the Normans controlled towns, river crossings and the meeting points of major roads, and could move around the country easily

Most castles were built with English forced labour, and the English were charged taxes to maintain them, adding to the feeling of Norman dominance.

The Anglo-Saxon Chronicle describes the Normans building castles everywhere, oppressing the unhappy local people and making things 'always go from bad to worse'.

Now try this

Describe **three** ways in which castles helped the Normans establish their rule in England.

Early revolts, 1067-68

Despite William's early attempts to win over the English earls, Norman rule was deeply unpopular.

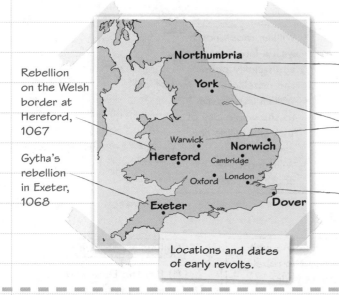

Rebellion on the Welsh border at Hereford, 1067

Gytha's rebellion in Exeter, 1068

Northumbria

York

Warwick

Hereford

Norwich

Cambridge

Oxford

London

Exeter

Dover

Rising in Northumbria, 1067

Edwin and Morcar's rebellion in Mercia and York, 1068

Rising in Kent, 1067

Locations and dates of early revolts.

Reasons for rebellion

- Some English people hated having foreigners ruling over them.
- Many Norman lords did not understand local customs.
- The more distant regions were harder to control.
- Many families lost land and titles after the Conquest, which caused resentment.
- Some people had lost relatives at Hastings and wanted revenge.
- William demanded high rates of tax, which caused poverty.

Rebellion on the Welsh border, 1067

The first large uprising against the Normans was in Mercia. It was led by an English thegn called Eadric.

Eadric had lost his land to Norman knights. He joined with two Welsh kings and attacked Hereford, destroying the city. William returned from Normandy. Eadric was never caught and continued his attacks.

Kent and Northumbria, 1067

The people of Kent were angry about their treatment by the Normans. They persuaded a former ally of William's, Eustace of Boulogne, to attack Dover. His attack failed and Eustace went home.

In Northumbria, William's chosen ruler, Copsig, was ambushed and murdered. William allowed Copsig's killer to take over.

Exeter, 1068

> King Harold's mother, Gytha, plotted rebellion in Exeter and challenged William's authority. She also tried to persuade the Danish king to invade England.

> William was furious and marched an army to besiege Exeter.

> The city surrendered after 18 days – Gytha and her family escaped.

> The rebels agreed to swear loyalty to William.

> William treated the rebels leniently, but he built a castle in Exeter and others around the south west.

Rebellion in Mercia and York, 1068

> Several English earls, including Edwin and Morcar, had submitted to William in order to keep their land and power.

> In 1068, they realised that their power was being chipped away so they led a revolt against William and several other English nobles joined them.

> William marched into Edwin's lands in Mercia, building a castle at Warwick and allowing his men to terrorise the population. He then moved north, building castles at Nottingham, York, Lincoln, Huntingdon and Cambridge.

> Edwin and Morcar again submitted to William, who pardoned them.

> William decided that he needed to put a trusted ally in charge of the north. He appointed Robert de Comines to the job.

This appointment triggered the next big rebellion. See page 12 for more.

Now try this

Write a paragraph to describe how William tried to deal with these early rebellions. Why do you think he chose to act in this way?

Further rebellion, 1069-75

Opposition to William's rule continued between 1069 and 1075.

Uprising in York

January 1069	February 1069
• Robert de Comines is appointed as the new earl of northern Northumbria. • Looting by his men triggers a rebellion in Durham: de Comines and his men are killed.	• An uprising in York: the governor and Norman troops are killed. • Edgar Ætheling comes down from Scotland to join the rebellion. • The Norman sheriff and his garrison are attacked.

• William races north with a large army and quickly ends the rebellion.
• William lays waste to the whole city of York and builds new castles.
• William returns south for Easter.

William was able to defeat the rebels in the north easily.

William entrusted York to William FitzOsbern while he went back to Winchester for Easter, to celebrate the festival as England's king.

The Danes attack York, September 1069

• King Sweyn of Denmark sends a large invasion fleet to England.
• The Danish invasion force meets up with Edgar Ætheling.
• 21 September: in the Anglo-Danish attack on York, 3000 Normans are killed.
• The Danes retreat to the Lincolnshire coast.

• William is in trouble. As well as the Danes and the rebels in the north, he is facing opposition elsewhere.
• New rebellions begin in Devon, Shrewsbury and Chester.
• As soon as William's forces subdue unrest in one region, it starts again somewhere else.
• The Danes bide their time, protected by marshland.

William's solutions

(1) Pay the Danes to leave England.

(2) The Harrying of the North.

(3) A symbolic show of power.

William had his crown sent to York and wore it to celebrate Christmas.

Hereward the Wake and rebellion at Ely

• Hereward had returned to Ely around 1069 from exile. He started a rebellion because he had lost his lands to a new Norman lord.
• In 1070 the Danes returned and set up base in Ely. The Danes and Hereward joined forces for a raid on Peterborough Abbey.
• Hereward had hoped to save the treasures of the monastery from the Normans, but the Danes took all the treasure and sailed back to Denmark with it.
• Morcar and his men came to Ely and joined Hereward. They defended Ely but the Normans eventually defeated them.
• Morcar was captured while Hereward escaped – but he was not heard of again.

In 1069, Harold's sons tried to invade the south west. They were unsuccessful, mainly because the city of Exeter refused to support them.

In 1072, Edgar Ætheling who had previously fled to Scotland sparked a revolt there, but it was easily put down.

Revolt of the earls, 1075

One further challenge came from the Normans.

Roger, Earl of Hereford (the son of William's friend William FitzOsbern) was angry at his reduced influence.

He plotted with another earl, Ralph de Gael, and the English earl Waltheof. The revolt was supported by the Danes.

William was able to defeat the rebellion entirely. Waltheof never joined in. The other two earls were cornered before they could attack.

Roger and Ralph lost their land. Waltheof was beheaded.

Now try this

Write a short paragraph explaining how the way William dealt with rebellions changed between 1067 and 1075. Why do you think this was?

The Harrying of the North

The Harrying of the North in 1069 showed that William was prepared to take extreme measures to keep England under his control.

Reasons for the Harrying
- To destroy the spirit of rebellion in the north.
- Revenge for the death of Robert de Comines and hundreds of other Normans.
- To prevent Vikings using Yorkshire as a base for future attacks.
- As a warning to other areas of England of what could happen to them.
- A military response to guerrilla warfare, which depended on support for rebels from local people.

The Harrying of the North as shown on the Bayeux Tapestry.

Features
- Homes destroyed so people had nowhere to shelter.
- Took place in the winter of 1069–70.
- Area of Harrying stretched from the Humber River to the Tees River. Also in Staffordshire and parts of Shropshire.
- Seed destroyed so there was nothing to plant for food the next year.
- Livestock killed.

Harrying of the North

Immediate consequences
- Death of thousands from starvation: perhaps as many as 100 000 people died.
- Flood of refugees from the north to other parts of England, for example, the west.
- Reports of families selling themselves into slavery to survive.
- Reports of cannibalism by desperate, starving people.

Long-term consequences
- No further rebellion from the north; after 1071 no further Anglo-Saxon rebellions.
- Danish invaders in 1070 went to Ely as there was now no base for them in Yorkshire
- A turning point: after 1070 William decided to replace the English aristocracy with Normans.
- Criticism of William's brutality and William's own sense of his sin and need for penance.
- 20 years later, Yorkshire had still not recovered; 60 per cent was listed as 'waste' in the Domesday Book and there were between 80 000 and 150 000 fewer people than in 1066.

Reasons for William's success
- William's soldiers were extremely effective against poorly armed rebels.
- William's methods were brutal, crushing immediate rebellion and making it impossible for new rebellions to break out.
- Opposition was not united making it easy for William to weaken them (for example by paying off the Danes).

The early medieval period was a violent time, but William's Harrying of the North was seen as especially brutal, even by his contemporaries. William was criticised by the pope for his actions, and was said to have repented for the deaths of so many people for the rest of his life.

Criticism of the Harrying of the North

The historian Orderic Vitalis was half English, half Norman. He often praised William but was very critical of the Harrying of the North and wrote the following in volume IV of *The Historia Ecclesiastica* between 1123 and 1131:

> For this act which condemned the innocent and guilty alike to die by slow starvation I cannot commend him. For when I think of helpless children, young men in the prime of life … I am so moved to pity that I would rather lament the grief and sufferings of the wretched people than make a vain attempt to flatter the perpetrator of such infamy.

Now try this

In no more than **three** sentences, explain why you think William wanted to make the north uninhabitable.

The Norman dynasty

After the earls' revolt in 1075, William's position in England was secure. This was not the case in Normandy, so he spent most of his time there. In 1087 he was injured at the Battle of Mantes and died six weeks later.

Another succession crisis?

Unlike Edward the Confessor, William had three sons, but it was not clear which one should be king.

1 William and his eldest son, Robert, did not get on well. Robert was heir to Normandy, but according to contemporaries, William thought he was 'proud and silly'.

2 Instead, William wanted his second son, William (known as 'Rufus'), to rule England. Robert was very unhappy about this.

3 William's third son, Henry, was left money but no land.

Although it wasn't clear which son would succeed William, it was accepted without question that England's next king would be a Norman.

Odo's rebellion

William Rufus arrived in England in September 1087 with a letter addressed to Lanfranc, the Archbishop of Canterbury. The letter said Lanfranc should help William Rufus.

⬇

William Rufus was crowned king (William II) by Lanfranc on 27 September 1087, but the following year, Bishop Odo of Bayeux plotted a rebellion with six leading barons.

⬇

The barons held land in England and Normandy and did not want to swear loyalty to two rulers (Robert was now Duke of Normandy).

⬇

William Rufus found out about the plot. He bought the barons off with promises (which he never kept). Odo surrendered and, in 1091, William Rufus and Robert settled their differences.

England in 1087

- William I had ruled both England and Normandy, so he relied on his followers to keep control of his kingdom. He did this through land ownership and by introducing the feudal system. This gave the king very secure control.

For more on the feudal system, see page 15.

- Many English people had opposed Norman rule and William had faced several rebellions. He was able to deal with this opposition using a variety of methods – such as concessions, patronage and intimidation – meaning that there had been no serious rebellion since 1075.

- Castles were a key part of ensuring Norman control of England – they maintained a military presence and were a powerful symbol of Norman domination.

- Although there was some difficulty over the succession when William died, showing that the nobles could still challenge the king, it was clear that the Norman grasp on England was secure.

Find out how William secured his control over the country on pages 15–20.

Silver coins with portraits of William II (William Rufus) and Henry I.

Henry I

William Rufus was killed in a hunting accident in August 1100. His younger brother Henry claimed the throne – so quickly that he was suspected of plotting his brother's death (although there is no proof of this). Henry agreed with his brother Robert that they would both keep to their own kingdoms. However, he went back on this and defeated Robert in battle in 1106 – meaning that he ruled both Normandy and England, just as his father, William I, had done.

Now try this

What do you think was the most important method William I used to secure control of England for the Norman dynasty? Give **three** reasons for your answer.

The feudal system

In Anglo-Saxon England, society was based on land ownership. William developed this system and made it more formal, thereby giving himself more power. This was called **feudalism**.

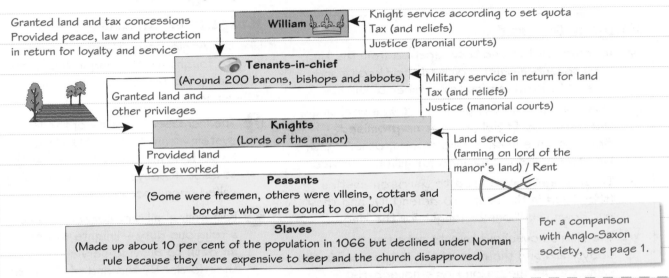

Granted land and tax concessions
Provided peace, law and protection
in return for loyalty and service

William 👑

Knight service according to set quota
Tax (and reliefs)
Justice (baronial courts)

Tenants-in-chief
(Around 200 barons, bishops and abbots)

Granted land and
other privileges

Military service in return for land
Tax (and reliefs)
Justice (manorial courts)

Knights
(Lords of the manor)

Provided land
to be worked

Land service
(farming on lord of the
manor's land) / Rent

Peasants
(Some were freemen, others were villeins, cottars and
bordars who were bound to one lord)

Slaves
(Made up about 10 per cent of the population in 1066 but declined under Norman
rule because they were expensive to keep and the church disapproved)

For a comparison
with Anglo-Saxon
society, see page 1.

Changes in land ownership

In 1065, about 4000 Anglo-Saxon thegns owned land. By 1086, land ownership was more concentrated and most of it was owned by Normans. This meant that the land was in the hands of people William could trust.

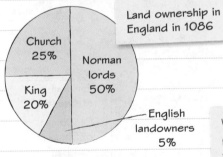

Land ownership in
England in 1086

Church 25%

Norman lords 50%

King 20%

English landowners 5%

Increased use of patronage

The feudal system – in which everyone depended on the king for their land – gave William enormous powers of **patronage**: controlling access to wealth and power meant that he had a very effective way of rewarding (or punishing) his followers.

William began to assert more control over his tenants. When a tenant died, he charged a fee, decided whether the tenant's widow could remarry, and controlled the land if there was no heir. This increased his powers of patronage even more.

Find out more about William's expansion of patronage on page 17.

William also learned from Edward the Confessor's mistakes – he made sure that none of his barons had too much land. This made it harder for them to build a power base and challenge the king.

Forest Law

William I loved hunting so he created huge hunting reserves, called Royal Forests. These forests had once been common land that everyone could use for hunting and grazing animals, but under the feudal system they belonged to the king. They were governed by **Forest Law** which meant that anyone caught hunting there risked severe punishments, for example, blinding.

Forest Law was extremely unpopular. The rich hated losing their ability to hunt for sport and the poor lost a vital source of food.

Key terms

- ✓ **Patronage** – controlling access to privileges, land or appointments.
- ✓ **Tenant-in-chief** – someone who held their fief (land) directly from the king.
- ✓ **Hierarchy** – a system where people are ranked by status.

Now try this

Describe **two** ways in which the feudal system differed from the Anglo-Saxon social hierarchy and **two** ways in which it was similar.

Military service

In 1067, William was ruling around two million people, most of whom were hostile. To keep control of his kingdom, he needed a supply of soldiers and the feudal system provided them.

Knights for land

- ✓ In return for the land they received from the king, each **tenant-in-chief** promised their loyalty and agreed to provide a certain number of knights.

- ✓ This commitment was binding – it was vital that the tenant could deliver what he promised. Some tenants-in-chief paid troops, others gave land to knights in exchange for military service.

- ✓ These knights were used to **garrison** castles (they lived in the castle to defend it), and they put down rebellions or fought for the king.

- ✓ The king's household knights acted as a bodyguard and the core of the king's army in the same way as the Saxon king's housecarls.

For more information on the role of housecarls, see page 7.

Knights vs thegns

Like the Anglo-Saxon thegns, Norman knights fought for the king in return for their land. However, there were some key differences:

1. The increased formality of the feudal system meant that knights always had to perform military service – usually at least 40 days – rather than being called upon when needed.

2. Performing military service was now a religious duty – knights **swore an oath** to provide service to their lords. By the end of the 12th century, there were 5000 knights who owed military service.

Securing the border with Wales

Wales was not a united country in the 11th century – it was ruled by five warrior princes. This meant that William could not conquer it in the same way he had conquered England, and the border between England and Wales (**the Marches**) was constantly under attack.

William didn't want any of his tenants-in-chief to become too powerful and restricted the amount of land they could hold. However, the Welsh Marches were an exception. He gave larger areas of land to his most trusted followers, the Earls of Chester, Shrewsbury and Hereford. These men became known as the **Marcher Lords**.

In return for protecting their areas from Welsh raids, the Marcher Lords could:

- keep their own armies
- build castles without William's permission
- make laws for their areas.

The Marcher Lords did attack parts of Wales and managed to claim some territory there, but they never had secure control over Wales.

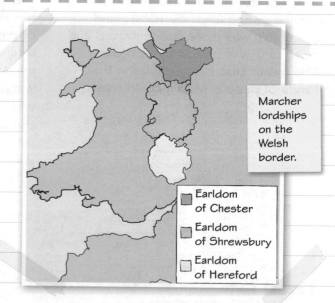

Marcher lordships on the Welsh border.

Earldom of Chester

Earldom of Shrewsbury

Earldom of Hereford

Securing the border with Scotland

In 1072, William tried to invade Scotland but was unsuccessful. There were frequent battles with the Scots over the border. The **Prince-Bishop of Durham** was given similar powers to the Marcher Lords in order to protect the border.

The **Treaty of Abernethy** in 1072 made King Malcolm III a client king of the Normans – although the two countries were theoretically at peace, border raids continued.

Now try this

Give **two** reasons why William made the system of military service more clearly structured.

Changes to government

The Anglo-Saxon system of government was efficient but William adapted it to increase his power.

Anglo-Saxon government

The king: Medieval kings were expected to be strong warriors, as well as wise and fair. The king:

- made laws for the whole kingdom
- raised taxes
- heard the most serious legal cases.

The Witan: Anglo-Saxon kings were advised by the Witan – the earls, other nobles and senior churchmen. The Witan did not limit the king's power – he did not have to follow their advice – but they were still an important group.

Government by writ: Anglo-Saxon kings used to issue writs – documents that set out their orders which were then sent around the country. The documents were written by royal clerks in the **Chancery**. The earls had a lot of power to decide how their earldoms were controlled.

Local government: To make sure his orders were carried out, the king needed an effective system of local government. Each shire had a 'capital' where justice and taxation was overseen by a shire-reeve (or sheriff). Shires were divided into smaller areas called 'hundreds'.

Norman changes

Difference: William extended the king's power, constantly reminding his subjects that he had God's approval. He also increased his power of patronage, which gave him more control over the lives of his subjects.

Similarity: William continued to seek the advice of his leading subjects through the **Curia Regis** (king's council).

Similarity: William continued to govern by writ, and he kept the Anglo-Saxon Chancery. **Difference:** He issued more orders than the Anglo-Saxon kings, and reduced his nobles' power to strengthen central control.

Similarity: William kept this system. The sheriff acted as the baron's deputy and as a link between the king and the shire. **Difference:** He slowly replaced English sheriffs with Normans – loyal sheriffs were vital to maintaining control. **Difference:** He also introduced new roles, such as castellans, who looked after royal castles and forests. The role of castellan might be performed by the lord or sheriff.

The Anglo-Saxons divided their property between their sons but the Normans introduced **primogeniture** (everything goes to the eldest son). Large estates were kept together, centralising power.

William introduced new laws called **feudal incidents**. If a tenant died without an heir, their land was returned to the lord, who could keep it, sell it or give it to someone else.

Inheritance

If a tenant died and his heir was underage, the lord could take over the land and keep the profits until the heir was old enough. The king owned the most land so he benefited the most – not only did he get more control over how land was passed on, it gave him an important new source of income.

Patronage

Patronage was an important way to ensure loyalty to the king. Disloyal subjects could expect to lose their land, or worse. Anyone wanting influence or land had to stay loyal to the king.

The feudal system meant that William could offer land in exchange for loyalty but he also made changes to government to increase his powers of patronage. The changes to the laws on inheritance meant that even after land was given, the king's favour was needed to pass it on.

Granting a sheriffdom ensured that the official was loyal directly to the king as well as to the baron he served.

For more on patronage, see page 15.

Now try this

List **three** features of Anglo-Saxon government that William kept, and **three** changes that he made.

The legal system

William kept a lot of the features of the Anglo-Saxon legal system. This was partly because it was an effective system, and partly because continuity helped to show that William's rule was legitimate.

How was the legal system structured?

The King's Court — Dealt with royal pleas for the serious crimes such as treason and murder, as well as appeals from lower courts. The king's judgement was final and binding.

Shire courts — Dated from Anglo-Saxon times and remained much the same under Norman rule. They were supervised by the sheriff and dealt with land disputes and crimes such as theft or assault.

Hundred courts — Were in place before the Conquest. They dealt with minor disputes and were overseen by a bailiff.

The Lord's (or honorial) courts — Were introduced by the Normans. Here, lords dealt with their tenants' disputes and cases of crime, supervised property transactions and announced new laws from the king. The lord also asked the tenants, who knew the land and people well, for advice when making decisions at court.

The manorial court — Was overseen by a lord of the manor (usually a knight) and dealt with everyday matters in the village, for example, complaints about bad work or applications to marry.

The Normans also introduced new church courts – you can find out about these on page 27.

How was the law enforced?

There was no police force in medieval times. Instead there were a number of different roles and systems for making sure people obeyed the law. These were all Anglo-Saxon systems that the Normans kept.

Constables could arrest people and break up fights. They were also responsible for preventing fires. They could put people in the stocks for minor offences. The job was not well paid so most constables had to do other work as well. The Normans appointed more constables and gave them more powers.

Most towns had a **watchman** who enforced the curfew (rules saying that people could not leave their homes at night). They were supposed to catch criminals, but as they weren't paid, they often didn't take the job very seriously.

Norman law enforcement

There was also a system called **tithing**, where a group of freemen promised to keep each other out of trouble. If one of them committed a crime, the rest had to report him – or the whole group would be punished.

See page 19 for information about trials and punishment.

If a crime was committed, the person discovering it had a duty to raise the alarm. Anyone hearing the alarm had to help catch the suspect. This was called the **hue and cry** – anyone ignoring it could be fined.

Now try this

William made very few changes to the Anglo-Saxon legal system. Give **two** reasons for this.

Trials and punishment

The Normans continued to use the Anglo-Saxon system of trials, but standardised it across the country with the system of sheriffs and honorial courts. They also introduced some changes to both trials and punishments.

Trials

Anglo-Saxon trials varied across the country. Although the watchmen and constables were there to catch criminals, cases were usually brought to court by the victim, or by one of the victim's relatives.

There was often very little evidence, so the courts looked for other ways to decide innocence or guilt.

Trial by cold water.

Trial by hot iron.

Types of trials

Trials used by Anglo-Saxons that died out during Norman times	Trials used by Anglo-Saxons that continued to be used by the Normans	Trials introduced by the Normans
Oaths People who knew the accused person were often asked to comment on his or her character. To ensure that they were honest, they had to swear an **oath** (a solemn promise) on a holy book or sacred relic.	**Trial by ordeal** This was used throughout medieval Europe before 1066. The accused would undergo an ordeal (usually administered by a priest). It was believed that God would protect the innocent. In **trial by cold water**, the accused was dunked into water (which the priest had blessed). It was believed that holy water would repel a sinner, so if the person floated, they were guilty. For **trial by hot iron**, the accused had to hold a piece of hot iron. Their hand would be bandaged and after three days, the wound was inspected. If it was clean, they were believed innocent; if it was infected, they were found guilty.	**Trial by battle** This was introduced by the Normans for use in serious cases. The accused and their accuser (or people they appointed to take their place) would fight with pointed sticks or swords. Again, the belief was that God would protect the person who was telling the truth. It was not necessarily a fight to the death, but if someone gave up they were admitting that they were in the wrong. Someone facing a death sentence might prefer to fight to the death than surrender and be executed.

Punishment

Punishments used by Anglo-Saxons that died out during Norman times	Punishments that increased during Norman times	Punishments introduced by the Normans
Under the Anglo-Saxons, if someone was found guilty of a less serious crime, such as theft, they would have to pay compensation to the victim. In cases of murder, the victim's family would have to be paid the **wergild** – the value of the person's life (which varied according to their rank). If the wergild was not paid the accused faced execution.  Wergild.	Physical punishments such as execution (hanging and beheading) and mutilation (maiming).  Maiming (corporal). Hanging (capital). Beheading (capital).	The **murdrum fine** meant that if a Norman was killed by an English person, the local community had five days to hand over the killer or face a heavy fine. The fine was charged until the killer was brought to justice, making murdrum an effective deterrent – anyone attacking a Norman knew that their chances of being caught were very high.

Now try this

Explain (in one or two sentences) what the introduction of the murdrum fine tells us about relations between the English and the Normans.

The Domesday Book

In 1085, William commissioned the Domesday Book to tell him what land and property there was, who owned it, and what it was worth. It confirmed William's rule and Norman ownership of England.

Commissioning the Domesday Book

- In December 1085, William met with his advisers. He ordered a survey listing all of the land and property in England, and details of who owned it.
- England's 34 shires were divided into seven regions (or **circuits**).
- There were four commissioners in each circuit. They visited every manor.
- In total, the commissioners visited 13 400 places.
- The 'Domesday Book' is actually two books. Essex, Norfolk and Suffolk are in 'Little Domesday'. 'Great Domesday' covers the rest of the kingdom, except London and areas that the king didn't control directly (for example, the parts of the north ruled by the Prince-Bishop of Durham).
- The whole survey was completed in under a year.

Inquests on land ownership

There had been many changes in land ownership since the Conquest. Some people had written proof that they owned land, but others didn't.

Special sessions of the shire court (inquests) heard evidence and made final, binding decisions about who owned the land. This would have been a stressful process.

William did not call it the 'Domesday Book'. It was kept in the Treasury in Winchester, so at first it was called the King's Book, the Book of the Treasury or the Book of Winchester. The name 'Domesday' was given later – it means the Day of Judgement. It meant that what was in the book was final.

What questions did the Commissioners ask?

1. **To start, they asked:**
   What is the name of the manor?
   How much land is there?

2. **What resources are there?**
   How many ploughs? Mills? Fisheries?

3. **What sort of land is it?**
   How much meadow? Woodland? Pasture?

4. **Who lives here?**
   How many freemen? Villeins? Slaves?

5. **Finally, they asked:**
   How much is the manor worth now?
   How much was it worth on the day King Edward died?

The uses of the Domesday Book

The Domesday Book established that the Normans were the legal owners of English land, and that William was the legitimate heir to Edward the Confessor. It also showed that everyone who held land did so through the king's authority.

The meeting which decided to carry out the Domesday survey had been called because of the threat of a new Viking invasion in 1085. Although the invasion never happened, it is possible William used the Domesday Book to see how many more knights his tenants could provide for knight service.

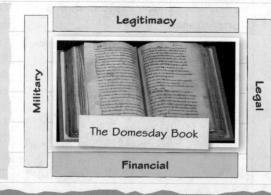

Legitimacy

Military

Legal

The Domesday Book

Financial

The Domesday Book contains records of claims by Anglo-Saxons that Normans had taken their lands. Since the Domesday surveys were made as fairly as possible, with key people from each hundred saying who owned what, the Domesday Book had a role in sorting out legal disputes.

The Domesday Book allowed the king to see where landholders should be paying more tax. The way it is organised also suggests that it was used to calculate feudal incidents, for example, to work out what fees should be charged when land was inherited.

See page 17 for more on feudal incidents.

Now try this

What was the main reason William chose to collect information about England in 1066 and 1086? Write a sentence explaining your view.

Villages

Day-to-day life in villages changed very little – most people were farming the land for a lord, and the work did not change even if the lord did. However, the Normans made several important changes.

Villages before 1066

Most people lived in the countryside and worked for a thegn in exchange for somewhere to live. The legal system was very much in favour of the landowner. The villagers grew crops and farmed animals, and were at the mercy of the harvest; a poor harvest led to starvation.

Each village was surrounded by large fields, which were divided into strips. Each villager was given a few strips to farm – this meant that good and bad land was shared equally. Villagers usually agreed together which crops to grow – wheat, rye and barley were the main crops.

Ploughing and other rural pursuits (11th century).

How did things change under the Normans?

Although the work people did stayed the same, village life changed in other ways:

- Land ownership – most villages found that their Saxon thegn was replaced with a Norman lord, who spoke French and followed different customs.

- In most cases, rents increased hugely – many freemen struggled to pay and had to become **villeins**.

- The Normans rebuilt many buildings in stone, including village churches. The increase in the number of parish priests meant that many villages which had not had a priest before 1066 now had one.

  > For more on the Church at this time, see pages 26–30.

- Many lords also built water mills – they charged the peasants to use the mill.

- Many villages were affected by Forest Law, which removed an important source of food.

  > To find out more about Forest Law, see page 15.

The farming year

Farming was hard work all year round – the work depended on the seasons. This diagram shows the main tasks. Many of these jobs were done by the whole family.

Winter
Butchering animals
Preserving meat
Digging ditches
Repairing buildings and tools

Spring
Ploughing
Sowing
Weeding
Pruning trees and bushes
Lambing/calving

Summer
Harvesting crops
Shearing sheep
Ploughing after harvesting
Collecting firewood
Fruit picking
Preserving fruit

Autumn
Finishing the harvest
Sowing
Milling
Making rope and baskets

The farming year in Norman England.

Peasants

Approximately 97 per cent of the population were peasants, but there were several types of peasant.

Freemen (the Anglo-Saxon ceorls) paid rent to the lord for their land. Sometimes they had to do work for the lord as well.

Villeins worked on the lord's land and were unpaid, although they were given a small amount of land to farm for themselves. They could not marry without the lord's permission and couldn't leave the village.

Bordars and **cottars** were also tied to the village. They were poorer and given less land by the lord.

Thralls (slaves) made up about 10 per cent of the population in 1066. Slavery fell rapidly under the Normans – possibly because the Church disapproved but more likely because it was cheaper to give land in return for labour than to support slaves.

Now try this

Do you think there was more change or more continuity in village life in Norman England? Give **three** reasons for your answer.

Had a look ☐ Nearly there ☐ Nailed it! ☐

Towns

Towns saw more significant changes than the countryside. Many towns grew in size and importance because of the potential for wealth.

Anglo-Saxon towns

There were very few towns in Anglo-Saxon England – those that existed were vital centres for the English wool trade. This meant that many towns grew on the south and east coasts.

Other towns grew where rivers or important roads crossed, making it easier for towns to specialise and then trade with each other.

Who lived in towns?

People came to towns to set up businesses, learn a trade as an apprentice, or to work as servants. If a villein managed to live in a town for a year and a day, he became a freeman.

Burgesses (citizens of towns) had more freedoms, and some legal protections. They also served as watchmen or in the town **militia**.

How a Norman town might have looked

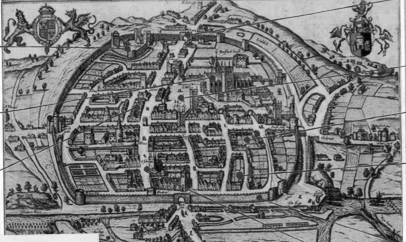

Castle

Church and/or monastery

Shops – usually along main street

This is a map of Exeter from slightly later than the Norman period but it still shows many of the features of a typical Norman town.

Gate guarded and locked at night

Market place

Residential houses

Workshops – often placed on the edge of town because of the smell and smoke some of them made

Town wall

Wide main street – width set by law

What changes did the Normans make to English towns?

Positive changes	Negative changes
👍 The Normans created 21 new towns. Most of these were founded because they were close to newly built castles, such as Ludlow in Shropshire.	👎 After the Conquest, towns in rebellious areas were attacked and damaged.
👍 Increased trade with Normandy meant that some towns grew larger, especially in the south.	👎 Castle building often meant the clearance of houses and workshops.
👍 The wool trade continued to grow, and increased trade with Flanders led to expanding port towns.	👎 The population of some large towns (for example Oxford, York) fell, either because rebellions were suppressed or because the effect of higher rents/charges damaged businesses.
👍 The Normans introduced guilds, which controlled trade, and regulated the quality of goods.	👎 The Normans took control of market trading and increased rents and tolls.

Now try this

Did life in towns get better or worse under the Normans? Give **two** reasons for your answer.

Food

There were huge differences between the diets of the rich and the poor in the 11th century. The food the poor ate changed very little after the Conquest. However, increased trade with Normandy meant that the rich had access to goods such as wine.

Food for the poor

Most people ate with their fingers. They may have used a knife to cut food, or a spoon to eat stew.

Food shortages were always a threat – a poor harvest put peasants at risk of starvation.

The poor ate rough rye bread. They had to pay to use the lord's ovens to bake it.

Most peasants kept cows or goats for milk and made cheese. They also kept hens for eggs.

The most common meal was a soup called **pottage** made from peas or beans.

Animals were valuable so meat was a treat. The only way to preserve meat was to smoke it. Salt was expensive, so salted meat was uncommon. Some peasants could fish in the sea or in rivers.

Peasants ate what they could grow themselves, so their diet was quite simple.

Water wasn't fit to drink so peasants drank milk and brewed weak beer – even children would drink this! They sometimes made cider (from apples) or mead (from honey).

Some peasants grew fruit. This was usually cooked or preserved, as it was thought that it was unhealthy to eat it raw.

Peasants ate bread made from rye. If rye got damp, a fungus grew on it that caused a disease called ergotism. This caused painful pustules and many sufferers had hallucinations. Until the fungus was discovered many centuries later, people thought ergotism was caused by demons.

Food for the rich

The rich ate a lot more meat – often roasted or made into pies. Most often, they ate birds such as woodcock, lark and blackbird, as well as boar, venison and pork. They even had swan or peacock on special occasions.

The rich ate from plates made from wood, pewter or silver. The poor used rough wooden bowls or a **trencher** – a crust of dry bread.

Apart from onions and leeks, the rich ate very few vegetables. Any fruit they ate was preserved in honey or made into pies.

The meat the rich ate was sometimes not very fresh – spices were used to disguise the taste. Spices had to be brought from Asia and were extremely expensive.

As well as ale, the rich would drink wine, often brought from France.

The rich ate more luxurious food than the poor.

The rich thought that dairy products were food for the poor so they ate very little of them.

The bread eaten by the rich was made from wheat instead of rye. They called it 'white bread' but it was like modern wholemeal bread.

> ## Now try this

Who do you think had a healthier diet, the rich or the poor? Explain your answer in a short paragraph.

Work

For most people, work did not change much after 1066. The sort of work people did depended on where they lived and how wealthy they were.

Work in villages – the poor

Most people in the countryside – men and women – were peasant farmers and worked the land, but there were other occupations:

- Millers – if the lord built a mill, there would be a miller. The miller was usually one of the richest people in the village.
- Blacksmiths – most villages needed a blacksmith to make and mend tools.
- Carpenters made things out of wood.
- Wagon-makers
- Wheelwrights made wheels.
- Weavers wove cloth.

Work in villages – the rich

- The lords did not do physical labour – their income came from the land that was farmed by their tenants. They did, however, have to spend time running their estates and overseeing the various courts they were responsible for while their wives ran the household.
- Knights were expected to perform military service and they also needed to train and practise their fighting skills and horsemanship.
- Sheriffs were responsible for administering the shire and overseeing the courts.

Jobs in a medieval town

The richest people were doctors, lawyers and merchants.
They usually owned property and served on town councils or acted as mayor.

Towns were important trading centres, so there was a wide range of craftsmen and tradesmen. Master craftsmen could earn a very good living. In most towns there would be:
- butchers, fishmongers, brewers and grocers selling food
- bakers – bread was a staple food so bakers were very important; sometimes people used the baker's oven to make their own bread
- tailors, robemakers and shoemakers
- masons (builders) and carpenters
- gold and silversmiths, armourers and potters
- apothecaries who sold medicines, herbs, spices and sugar
- barbers who cut hair, pulled teeth and performed surgery and even amputation
- blacksmiths who made iron goods such as tools, hinges, keys, gates and weapons
- gongfermers who emptied cesspits, usually at night.

The poorest people were the domestic servants and unskilled labourers – they had to find work where they could and their life was very uncertain.

Learning a trade

Moving to a town to learn a trade gave people a chance at a better lifestyle. However, it was not easy.

⬇

An apprentice (usually a teenage boy) would agree to work for a master craftsman for seven years in exchange for housing, clothing and food.

⬇

Once he finished his apprenticeship, he would become a **journeyman** and be paid wages.

⬇

Eventually, he could become a master by showing his skills in a **masterpiece** (a special piece of work).

Women's work in towns

We know less about women's work in the Middle Ages than we do about men's work.

The guilds did not allow women to learn most trades, but many women worked alongside their male relatives and were occasionally allowed to inherit the business when the craftsman died. Some of these women became very successful.

However, most women worked as domestic servants, laundresses and brewers. In addition to their daily work, women ran their households, raised their children and craftsmen's wives often supervised apprentices.

Now try this

Suggest **one** advantage of working in a town and **one** disadvantage.

Housing

Most houses were built of wood – only the very rich had stone houses. Most people's homes were damp, dark and smoky.

Village houses

The village would have been dominated by the manor house, where the lord lived. The Anglo-Saxon thegn's hall (which would have been built out of wood) was replaced with a stone house. Around the manor house were barns, which were shared with the whole village.

The rest of the houses in the village were the peasants' homes. The largest belonged to the freemen.

The villeins' houses were smaller and each had a plot of land where they could grow vegetables and keep animals and poultry. The cottars and bordars had smaller plots of land.

There was a hole in the roof to let smoke escape

A peasant's house.

Everyone slept together in one room

No windows so house was very dark

Animals were brought into the house at night

The floor was earth covered with straw or rushes

Poor housing was one of the factors that led to a low life expectancy. Average life expectancy in the 11th century was only 30 years, because so many children died in infancy. If someone made it to adulthood, reaching their early sixties meant they had had a long life.

Housing in towns

Medieval town house with shop front.

Most houses were built out of wood and packed closely together. This made the streets very narrow.

Sometimes towns were built on a **grid structure**, but they were usually not very well planned. This meant that houses were fitted in where there was space.

Because land was so expensive, many houses were bigger above the ground floor. This meant that they overhung the street, which made the streets dark.

The ground floor of many houses on the high street served as shops for merchants and craftsmen, or as alehouses. The upper floors would often be shared between several families.

The high street was wider – it had to be the width of a **lance**. Any houses that narrowed the high street were knocked down!

Towns were overcrowded and there was no sewage system, meaning that disease spread quickly.

Wooden houses and the presence of craftsmen meant that there was a high risk of fire.

Most towns were surrounded by walls to keep people safe – this meant that space inside the town was limited. On the edge of the town, there were often larger houses, some with gardens – these were for the wealthy.

You will need to refer to page 24 and this page to answer this question.

Now try this

How do you think the Norman changes to towns affected the housing situation? Give **two** reasons for your answer.

The Anglo-Saxon Church

In 21st-century Britain, religion is a matter of personal choice. Some people are Christian, some belong to other faiths and some aren't religious at all. It was very different in the Middle Ages.

The influence of the Church in the Middle Ages

1 People believed that kings ruled by 'divine right' – that they were chosen by God. William was pious and would have wanted to show that he had God's favour by making sure his people followed church teachings.

2 Everyone was very concerned with what would happen when they died. The Day of Judgement and whether they went to heaven or hell was of major, everyday importance.

3 Following the teachings of the Church was vital if you wanted to go to heaven – and the Church made rules about every aspect of life, down to what people could eat.

4 Every village had a priest, and everyone was expected to go to Mass (the main church service) and follow the priest's instructions.

5 Religious leaders – such as bishops – were as wealthy and powerful as nobles.

6 The leader of the Church, the pope, was probably the most powerful man in Europe.

An Anglo-Saxon church in the town of Bradford on Avon, Wiltshire. Surviving Anglo-Saxon churches are rare because few were made of stone.

Understanding the importance of religion in this period is essential if you're going to grasp this topic.

Most people gave money to the Church without question because the Church was their only route to heaven. This made the Church very rich.

Largest landowner in England – collected a huge amount of rent

Fees were charged for funerals, weddings and baptisms

Where the Anglo-Saxon Church got its wealth

Church taxes were charged throughout the year

Tithes – everyone had to pay a tenth of their income to the Church

Legacies – people left their land and money to the Church

Criticisms of the Anglo-Saxon Church

The pope thought that the English Church was backward and corrupt, because:

- many priests broke Church rules by committing **pluralism** (holding two positions at once) and **simony** (selling off Church posts)
- many priests were married
- the English Church used English as well as Latin
- compared to priests in the rest of Europe, English priests were poorly educated.

Stigand became very rich and seemed to be very concerned with his own wealth and status. The pope insisted Stigand gave up one of his posts, but Stigand took no notice.

Archbishop Stigand

Stigand became Archbishop of Canterbury in 1052 and was an example of where the Anglo-Saxon Church was out of step with the rest of Europe and an irritation to the pope. Stigand was a skilled administrator but not particularly religious. He concentrated on advising the king rather than reforming the Church. He broke several Church rules (including committing pluralism and simony), but kept his position because Harold Godwinson supported him.

Now try this

Give **two** reasons why William the Conqueror may have wanted to reform the English Church when he took control in 1066.

Lanfranc and Church reforms

William had promised the pope that he would reform the English Church. Once his throne was secure, he appointed Lanfranc as Archbishop of Canterbury to carry out these reforms.

Battle for primacy

Once Lanfranc was appointed Archbishop of Canterbury, he had to establish his position. Thomas, Archbishop of York, argued that he had **primacy** (was the leader of the English Church).

⬇

York was a powerful **diocese** (the area run by a bishop); the Archbishop of York had crowned William. Lanfranc was a scholar and teacher, and he had William's backing.

⬇

Lanfranc refused to **consecrate** (ordain) Thomas unless he swore loyalty to him. Thomas refused until William ordered him to submit.

⬇

Thomas later complained to the pope, who refused to get involved – again, William pressured Thomas to accept Lanfranc's leadership.

Lanfranc

Timeline

1005 Born in Italy

1039 Became a teacher in France

1042 Became a monk at Bec Abbey in France and lived in seclusion for three years

1045 Opened a school and became a respected teacher

1066 Was appointed Abbot of St Etienne in Caen

1070 Was appointed Archbishop of Canterbury by William

A stained-glass window showing Lanfranc.

Lanfranc's reforms

1. **Synods** (Church councils) run by bishops were set up to spread reform.

2. Cathedrals were moved to bigger towns and cities to centralise the Church.

3. A new Church hierarchy was introduced to centralise the Church and give bishops more control over their dioceses.

4. The role of the parish priest was developed and numbers rose.

5. Clergy were no longer allowed to marry.

6. Lanfranc ended abuses such as simony and **nepotism** (favouring relatives).

The new church hierarchy

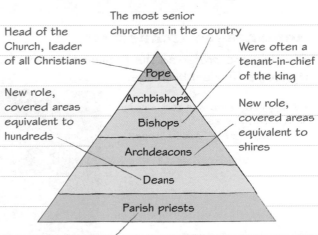

Head of the Church, leader of all Christians — Pope

The most senior churchmen in the country — Archbishops

Were often a tenant-in-chief of the king

New role, covered areas equivalent to hundreds — Archdeacons

New role, covered areas equivalent to shires — Bishops

Deans

Parish priests

The number of parish churches doubled in the century after the Conquest

Church courts

Church courts weakened his authority, but William supported Lanfranc.

In 1076, Lanfranc set up special Church courts. This meant that churchmen would now be tried in the bishop's courts (part of the synod) instead of the normal secular (non-religious) courts.

- Lanfranc believed that the secular courts didn't have the authority to try clergymen. This caused some resentment, as the secular courts gave out harsher punishments than the Church courts.

- As well as trying the clergy, Lanfranc wanted Church courts to deal with 'spiritual offences' (such as blasphemy, non-attendance at church or adultery) among ordinary people.

Now try this

Why was the close relationship between William and Lanfranc important? Give **two** reasons for your answer.

Church building

Alongside the reform of the English Church, William and Lanfranc began to replace England's church buildings.

Churches and cathedrals

One of the most visible changes made by the Normans was to England's churches and – especially – cathedrals.

England was a wealthy country so it could afford to buy the materials needed for rebuilding on a large scale. English forced labour was often used to carry out the building work. By the end of the 12th century, Westminster Abbey was the only Anglo-Saxon cathedral that had not been knocked down and rebuilt in the Norman style.

In addition, many Anglo-Saxon parish churches, which were usually simple wooden buildings, were replaced by more elaborate stone churches. Most churches dedicated to English saints were renamed.

New churches were also built in villages that had not previously had one – the number of churches doubled in the 100 years after the Norman Conquest.

Why did the Normans rebuild England's churches?

1. Normandy was famous for its beautiful churches – the Normans thought that Anglo-Saxon churches were old fashioned. William of St Calais ordered that Durham Cathedral be rebuilt on a 'nobler and grander scale'.

2. New religious buildings showed that God favoured Norman rule and that William was the legitimate monarch.

3. Organisational changes, such as moving bishops to important towns, meant that new cathedrals were required.

4. Magnificent churches and cathedrals were a powerful symbol of prestige – another way of reminding the English that the Normans were in charge.

Romanesque architecture

The Normans preferred the Romanesque architectural style – it combined features of Roman and Byzantine (Turkish) buildings.

The churches were well built – many survive to the present day – with thick walls and high quality stone.

One of the key features was rounded arches, which were used for doors and windows.

Many Romanesque churches had sturdy pillars and square towers.

Romanesque buildings were symmetrical and featured clean lines, giving them a simple appearance.

The Abbaye aux Dames in Caen, Normandy, was built by William the Conqueror and his wife Matilda in 1062. This was one of two cathedrals William built in Caen – the other one was called Abbaye aux Hommes.

Now try this

Give **two** ways in which new church buildings demonstrated Norman power.

William II and the Church

Lanfranc had been a close friend of William I. He had helped William II (also called William Rufus) succeed his father. However, William Rufus had a very different view of the Church from William I, and there was soon conflict.

William I vs William Rufus

William I was a genuinely religious man.	William Rufus did not appear to be religious at all.
William I had supported reform of the Church to reduce abuses.	William Rufus seemed more interested in making money from the Church.
The Church approved of William I.	The Church disapproved of William Rufus' morals. He never married and it is likely that he was homosexual.

Conflict with William of St Calais

In 1088, William of St Calais, the Bishop of Durham, told William Rufus about a plot against him and agreed to send troops to help.

He then changed his mind and didn't send troops after all. William Rufus was furious and had St Calais charged with treason.

St Calais said that he had the right to be tried in the Church courts. William Rufus refused. He said St Calais had broken his oath of fealty and should be tried in the king's court.

The trial took place in November 1088 in a secular court. St Calais was swiftly found guilty, and was sent into exile.

This is significant because:
- it showed that William Rufus was going to control the Church
- the nobles and clergy had supported the king
- it would have put off other people from challenging William Rufus.

Conflict with Archbishop Anselm and the Council of Rockingham

Lanfranc died in 1089. William Rufus did not replace him because he wanted to keep the income from Lanfranc's church estates.

In 1093, William Rufus became very ill. He was convinced that God was punishing him and decided to appoint a new Archbishop. He chose a pupil of Lanfranc's, a monk called Anselm.

This meant the relationship between William Rufus and Anselm was difficult from the beginning. Anselm openly criticised William Rufus' poor morals and his practice of keeping bishoprics empty so that he could keep the income.

Anselm refused at first. He only took the job on condition that Lanfranc's lands were given back to the Church, that he became William Rufus' spiritual adviser, and that William Rufus continued to recognise the pope's authority. Rufus agreed to this – except for giving back the lands.

Anselm had wanted to go to Rome to claim his **pallium** (a vestment that the pope gave to bishops to confirm that they had his blessing).

William Rufus wanted to reduce the pope's influence and felt that Anselm going to Rome was really a way of showing his allegiance to the pope. He refused to let Anselm go.

This compromise didn't last for long. William Rufus blocked Anselm's plans to reform the Church and Anselm did not want to pay extra taxes or provide knights.

The Council of Rockingham was called in 1095 to settle the dispute but the two sides could not agree. Eventually, William Rufus sent a message to the pope to ask for Anselm's pallium. When it arrived, it was presented to Anselm.

In 1097, Anselm was exiled and Rufus claimed the income from an empty post.

Now try this

Give **three** reasons why the Church criticised William Rufus.

Relations with the Papacy

The pope was incredibly powerful. All Christians were supposed to obey him, which meant that sometimes there were tensions between the pope and monarchs.

William I and the Papacy

1 Anglo-Saxon kings had very distant relations with the pope. William I wanted to change this. Pope Alexander II had supported William's invasion of England and given him the Papal Banner.

2 Like the pope, William saw the English Church as backward and corrupt, and wanted it to be reformed.

3 Pope Alexander II wanted corrupt bishops replaced, and William was happy to have an excuse to replace English bishops with Normans.

4 In 1073, Gregory VII became pope. He wanted more direct control over the running of the Church.

5 Pope Gregory VII wanted bishops to go to Rome to report to him, and he wanted William to swear fealty to him. William was not prepared to do this. Relations between the king and the pope began to decline.

William Rufus and the Papacy

1 William Rufus was not popular with the English Church. His relationship with the Papacy was no better.

For more on William Rufus' relationship with the Church, see page 29.

2 Pope Gregory VII wanted to be able to appoint bishops. However, many rulers, including William Rufus, objected to this and Pope Gregory was replaced with Pope Urban II.

3 William Rufus grudgingly accepted Urban as pope and, in return, Pope Urban II promised to stay out of English affairs – but the relationship between them was very frosty.

Pope Urban II consecrating the altar of the church of Cluny Abbey in France in 1085.

Henry I and the investiture controversy

Henry I became king in 1100 after his brother William Rufus died in a riding accident. He set out to improve relations with the Church by filling vacant offices and promising to end Church abuses. He also invited Anselm to return to his archbishopric.

⬇

However, Henry came into conflict with the pope over the issue of 'lay investiture'.

⬇

The pope also said that he did not want churchmen to pay homage to the king. Henry objected to this because the bishops were his tenants-in-chief – if they didn't pay homage, it would damage his authority.

⬇

Anselm refused to be invested by Henry and refused to pay homage to him. In 1103, he was exiled again. The pope threatened to **excommunicate** Henry (ban him from taking communion).

⬇

In 1107, a compromise was agreed in the Concordat of London. This said that Henry would give up his rights to invest bishops, but could still demand homage in exchange for their lands before they were consecrated.

Lay investiture meant that a lay person (a non-churchman, in this case, the king) would 'invest' (officially appoint) a newly consecrated bishop by presenting the symbols of his office. The pope objected to the idea that bishops relied on kings for their power and wanted an end to lay investiture.

Now try this

Give reasons why relations between the pope and the king sometimes became difficult.

Monastic reform

There had been monasteries in England since the 5th century, but during the 10th century the number of monks and nuns fell, and standards in the monasteries dropped. The Normans wanted to revive monasticism in England and introduce reforms.

What is monasticism?

 A **monastery** is a religious house where monks or nuns live a religious life. The religious way of life in a monastery is known as **monasticism**. In the medieval period, religion was of central importance and people thought that it was essential to have monks and nuns to pray for them. Praying was the main occupation of monks and nuns.

 Monasteries were also centres of learning – monks were some of the most educated people in England. Before the invention of the printing press, books were written by hand, usually by monks. They also ran schools.

 Monasteries provided accommodation for travellers.

 Monasteries gave money to the poor.

Monasteries looked after the sick.

The Rule of St Benedict

In the 6th century, St Benedict wrote rules about how monks should live.

Benedictine Rule

Poverty – giving up paid positions

Chastity – not getting married and being celibate

Obedience – obeying the abbot or prioress

Simplicity – wearing simple clothes (a habit) and eating two simple vegetarian meals a day

Prayer – attending eight prayer services a day

Work – everything they needed or ate had to be produced by them

Silence – apart from during prayer

Service – looking after the sick, poor and travellers

Monasteries depended on local lords for land and money. This gave the lords a lot of influence over the monastery – sometimes they even chose the abbot.

There had been a decline in monasteries throughout the 10th century, largely caused by Viking raids.

Why did the Normans want to reform English monasteries?

Standards in Anglo-Saxon monasteries had dropped – many monks were not observing all the services.

Many monasteries were very wealthy and monks lived in luxury, which was against the Benedictine Rule.

Lanfranc's monastic reforms

In 1077, Lanfranc introduced his reforms, which were designed to make sure that all monasteries were held to the same standards:

1 A new **liturgy** (the words of the service) that was closer to the one used in the rest of Europe.

2 A new hierarchy with clearly defined roles.

3 New, strict rules about the creation of saints (the English Church had previously ignored the pope's instruction that he had to approve new saints).

4 A new set of rules about how monks and nuns should live, bringing them back in line with the Rule of St Benedict.

Anglo-Saxon monastic leaders were replaced by Normans – by 1086, there were only three Anglo-Saxon abbots in England.

For more on Lanfranc, see page 27.

An English monk, Eadwine, at work on a manuscript in the 12th century.

Now try this

Suggest **one** reason why Lanfranc wanted to make all monasteries follow the same rules.

New monastic orders

The Norman reform and revival of monasticism meant that between 1066 and 1135, the number of monasteries increased from around 60 to more than 250. This was largely due to the growth of new monastic orders such as Cluniac monasteries.

The Rule of St Benedict was applied very strictly at Cluny.

The Cluniacs recruited 'lay brothers' to do the manual work, leaving monks free to concentrate on prayer and learning.

Pope Gregory VII (1073–85) asked the Abbot of Cluny to reform religious houses in Rome, then in France, and then elsewhere in Europe.

Some religious houses opposed the reforms, but others were keen to have help from the Cluniacs.

The Benedictine abbey at Cluny in France was founded in 910 and soon developed its own identity. The local duke had exempted the abbey from feudal duties, and the abbey answered directly to the pope.

Why Cluniac monasteries were different

The pope soon realised that Cluny's independence and piety could revive monasticism.

Why Cluniac monasteries were influential

Cluny became very important and very wealthy – this eventually caused criticism of the Cluniac order and by 1100 there were new orders that were stricter.

Most Benedictine monasteries were independent abbeys, overseen by an abbot. However, Cluniac monasteries were all priories and had no abbot, so reported directly to the Abbot of Cluny.

Cluniac monasteries and their impact

The spread of these new, stricter monasteries showed the importance of monastic discipline to the Normans.

The impact of Cluniac monasteries in England

Norman landowners often built monasteries or priories next to their castles to increase their prestige and to show that Norman rule was blessed by God. The pairing of the new castles and the new priories would have made a very clear statement of military and spiritual domination.

William and Lanfranc thought that the Cluniacs' discipline would help to improve monastic standards in England.

The Normans encouraged Cluniac priories in England. The first was built at Lewes in 1077. By 1135, there were 24 Cluniac priories in England.

The Cistercians and the Northern Revival

1. The Cistercian order was founded in France in 1098 by monks who thought the Cluniacs weren't strict enough.

2. In 1128, in the reign of Henry I, the first Cistercian house was founded in England at Waverley in Surrey.

3. Cistercians lived an austere life. They wore white robes, and preferred to settle in remote places and cultivate wild land.

4. This meant that many Cistercians settled in remote places in the north of England, causing what is known as the 'Northern Revival' of monasticism. The first major house was Rievaulx in Yorkshire.

5. The order farmed sheep and were important in the wool trade, becoming very wealthy and successful.

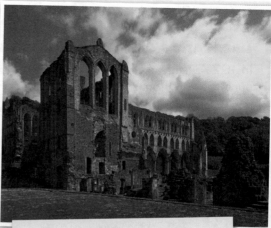

Rievaulx Abbey was one of the largest Cistercian abbeys in England.

You may want to look at page 31 to help you answer this question.

Now try this

Give **two** ways that Cluniac priories were important to the Norman revival and reform of monasticism.

Monastic life

Church reformers wanted monasticism to return to a simple life of prayer, work and study. They thought English monks were lazy and undisciplined, as many didn't follow the proper routine of services.

Daily life in a monastery

2 am	Matins, the first service of the day
5 am	Lauds, the early morning service
6 am	The service of Prime followed straight from Lauds
After Lauds	Work/study
9 am	Back to church for Terce, another service
After Terce	Chapter – a meeting in the chapter house where the business of the monastery was discussed
After Chapter	Work
Noon	The midday service was called Sext
After Sext	Main meal
3 pm	Nones, the afternoon service
After Nones	Work
5 pm	The evening service, Vespers, was recited before dark, so this would happen later in the summer
After Vespers	Supper, then reading and study
7 pm	Compline, the last service of the day, followed by bed

A bell would ring to wake the monks for Matins. They would go back to bed afterwards.

The abbot or prior would hold the meeting. Problems were discussed and tasks given out. **Confession** (confessing your sins) and **penance** (something you did to seek forgiveness) were very important, and this happened in Chapter.

The liturgy was changed from English to Latin, which many monks resented.

This was a simple, vegetarian meal – unlike the rich food many monks had been eating.

Monks were among the most educated people in society. Sometimes the Bible would be read aloud.

This is a typical timetable – they varied between monasteries. Vespers and Compline often happened later than this in the summer so that monks could make better use of daylight for work or study.

A typical monastery in Norman England

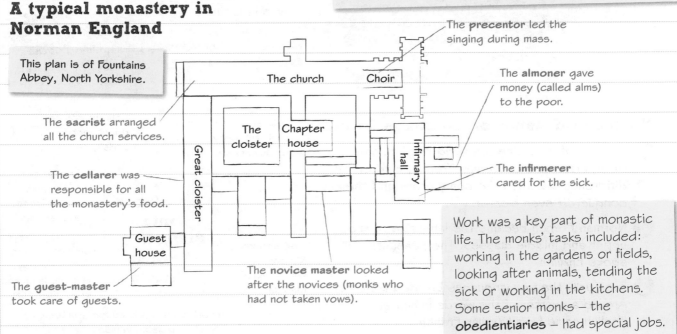

This plan is of Fountains Abbey, North Yorkshire.

The **precentor** led the singing during mass.

The church

Choir

The **almoner** gave money (called alms) to the poor.

The **sacrist** arranged all the church services.

The cloister

Chapter house

Great cloister

Infirmary hall

The **infirmerer** cared for the sick.

The **cellarer** was responsible for all the monastery's food.

Guest house

The **guest-master** took care of guests.

The **novice master** looked after the novices (monks who had not taken vows).

Work was a key part of monastic life. The monks' tasks included: working in the gardens or fields, looking after animals, tending the sick or working in the kitchens. Some senior monks – the **obedientiaries** – had special jobs.

Now try this

Suggest **two** reasons that English monks resisted the Norman changes to monastic life.

Learning and language

Before 1066, everyone in England spoke the same language. One of the biggest changes the Norman Conquest made was to language.

Before the printing press, books had to be handwritten – a bible could take more than a year. Monks copied texts in a special room called a 'scriptorium'.

Monasteries were some of the few providers of education – this was expensive so most people could not afford it.

Role of monasteries as centres of learning

Since Anglo-Saxon times, monks had kept historical records, such as the Anglo-Saxon Chronicle. Orderic Vitalis and William of Malmesbury were important chroniclers.

Schools and education

Education was mainly designed to train students to be priests or monks, so the curriculum included:

- Latin – the language of Church services and documents
- arithmetic – to run monastery accounts
- astronomy – to work out the Church calendar
- music – many Church services were sung
- law – to run the Church courts.

By 1100, all cathedrals had a school attached. Some members of the nobility sent their sons to Church schools, and they received a slightly broader education. Girls rarely received any education – a few learned to read and write but that was all.

An 11th-century document written in Latin.

Norman influence on language: Latin

Before the Conquest, most manuscripts were written in English. This stopped in 1066.

The language spoken by most people in a country or area is called the **vernacular** – in the case of England, the vernacular is another way of saying 'English'.

1. After 1066, William kept the Anglo-Saxon system of government by writ but changed the language of government from English to Latin.

2. When the Domesday survey was carried out, it was written in Latin.

3. The Anglo-Saxon Church had used English but the new liturgy introduced by Lanfranc was in Latin.

We know that some monks complained about having to translate their documents into Latin.

Norman influence on language: French

1. Instead of everyone speaking English, the ruling class spoke Norman French, making the difference between the conquerors and the conquered even clearer.

2. Norman French became the language of the upper and middle classes. The peasants still spoke English.

3. Eventually the two languages blended together. Around a quarter of the words in modern English came from Norman French.

Words introduced into English via Norman French

Politics: government, royal, authority, parliament, sovereign

Church: prayer, priest, abbey, parish, cemetery

Law: justice, court, jury, fraud, judge, accuse, appeal

First names: Richard, Robert, William, Alice, Matilda

Culture: dance, music, melody, fashion, language, poet, literature

Food: beef, pork, bacon, mutton, poultry, pigeon, venison

Now try this

You may find it useful to think about feudalism – see page 15.

Which do you think had more impact on most English people in Norman England – the introduction of Latin, or the introduction of French? Write a paragraph to explain your ideas.

 ## Site investigation

You will study **one** particular Norman site in depth. This site will be linked to the rest of your British depth study on Norman England. You will be told which site you are studying, and you will consider a range of information and resources connected with the site. There are seven key aspects about your site (as numbered below) that you need to consider. You need to learn facts about these key aspects and you need an understanding of the site's historical context.

Context and second order concepts

Remember to consider the wider historical **context**: What's the background to the site?

You also need to explore the following second-order concepts in relation to your site:

- ✓ **Change** – How has the site changed from earlier periods?
- ✓ **Continuity** – How has the site stayed the same?
- ✓ **Causation** – What caused the change? Why did things stay the same?
- ✓ **Consequence** – What are the consequences?

> Look out for links between the key aspects, too!

1 Location

Make sure you understand your site's **location**: Where is it? Why is it there? What is nearby? Is it near a town? On the coast? On an important road? Was it built on an existing site?

2 Function

Find out about your site's **function**: What was it used for? Did people live there? Was it built for military purposes? Was it used to show wealth and status? Was it a religious building?

3 Structure

What are the key facts about the **structure** of your site? Think about the key areas or features of the site, and where they are located within the site.

> For example, if your site is a castle, does it have a motte? Is there a tower? If your site is a monastery, where are the dormitories, church and chapterhouse?

4 People

Explore the full range of **people** connected with your site. For example: Who built it? Who lived there? Who visited it? Who worked there?

> Think about how people lived at the time. How were they governed? What were their beliefs and values? How did these differ between the Normans and the English?

5 Design

- How does the design reflect the site's purpose?
- What is the style of the architecture? What influences were there on the design?
- How does the design reflect who was in power at the time?
- How does the design reflect the values of the society at the time?
- What was it built from?

6 Culture, values and fashions

- How does your site reflect the **culture** and **fashion** of the day? For example, if your site is a cathedral, what style of architecture was used?
- How far does it reflect Norman social order and status? For example, if your site is a town, what types of buildings were there?

7 Important events and developments

Think about what was happening in England at the time and how your site links in with key events: for example, rebellions against Norman rule or Norman Church reforms.

Now try this

Write down **one** fact about the site you are studying for each of the seven key aspects above.

35

⦿ Site investigation

Sample site: Ely Cathedral 1

Have a look at the seven key aspects on page 35. This page and the next give you examples of each aspect for one sample site, as well as examples of change, continuity and causation.

Watch out: you will not be considering Ely Cathedral in your exam, so you don't need to learn these facts. You will need to make notes on the seven aspects for **your** selected site.

Context

Ely Cathedral was built by the Normans. It was part of the Norman programme to rebuild cathedrals and monasteries. Before the rebuilding, Ely Cathedral had been the church for an important Benedictine abbey. Work started in 1083 and Ely was given cathedral status in 1109.

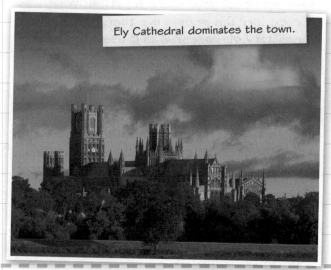

Ely Cathedral dominates the town.

1 Location

Ely Cathedral is located in Cambridgeshire, East Anglia. Ely is in a marshy region called the Fens. During the Norman period, the town was an island in the marsh. The cathedral is known as the 'Ship of the Fens' because the flat landscape means it is visible from a long distance.

Continuity   Ely Cathedral was built on the site of an abbey dating from the seventh century.

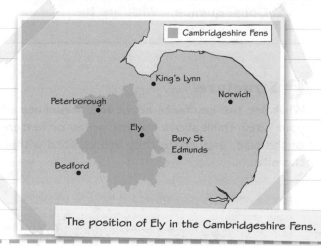

The position of Ely in the Cambridgeshire Fens.

2 Function

The cathedral was built as a place of worship, originally as the abbey church. Many cathedrals were built in important towns but during the Norman period, Ely was a small settlement.

The cathedral was built by the Benedictines who lived at the abbey – a large, elaborate building was a way to glorify God.

Causation   However, there was another reason. The Normans were rebuilding cathedrals and abbeys, and the monks of Ely knew that if they wanted to keep their status, they needed a grand new building.

3 Structure

• The cathedral was built to a **cruciform** (cross-shaped) design, with a tower, aisled transepts and a semi-circular apse at one end.

• It was one of the largest buildings in northern Europe when it was built.

• The walls are thick and made of stone with rounded arches – a key feature of the Romanesque architecture preferred by the Normans.

See page 37 for more about style and design.

Change   As well as building the church, the Normans also rebuilt the monastic buildings. However, these buildings were replaced in the later Middle Ages, so there's now no trace of them.

─ ─ **Now try this** ─ ─   You could also refer to page 37 to help you answer this question.

Describe **two** features of Ely Cathedral that indicate that it was intended to show prestige.

Site investigation # Sample site: Ely Cathedral 2

Make sure you have revised pages 35 and 36 before looking at this page.

4 People

- The building of the cathedral was supervised by Abbot Simeon, who became abbot of Ely in 1082. Simeon was a relative of William I.

- The abbey was a Benedictine house and the monks were mainly English. Before Simeon took over, the abbey had been involved in the rebellion of Hereward the Wake.

- Monks lived in the abbey and worshipped in the cathedral.

- The church was a place of worship for local people – the building of a large church would have been a powerful sign of Norman rule.

- There was a shrine to St Etheldreda, the founder of the abbey, which attracted pilgrims.

For more about the cathedral's function, see page 36.

5 Design

Marble decoration
Wooden roof
Romanesque style
Three tiers of rounded arches
Key features
Thick strong walls
Ely Cathedral

Its impact as a large and imposing building

Reflected power of the Normans constructing such magnificent buildings

Reflected high regard people had for God

The nave of Ely Cathedral shows key features of Romanesque architecture.

Continuity **Change** The monastic buildings and parts of the church were built in the early Gothic style in the later medieval period, but key Norman features remain.

6 Culture, values and fashions

The use of Romanesque style of architecture brought to England by Normans from France

Fashion

Ely Cathedral

Culture

Although they are now gone, the rebuilding of new abbey buildings reflects Norman monastic reform

Values

A large church shows how important religion was to people at the time

A cathedral would have been a huge display of wealth – most people lived in small wooden houses

7 Important events and developments

Ely Abbey suffered at the start of William I's reign.

Abbey lands were given to Normans.

The abbey's status was undermined by new Norman bishops.

In 1071, Ely was the centre of Hereward the Wake's rebellion and the siege of Ely. The abbey was heavily fined for its involvement in the rebellion.

For more on Hereward the Wake's rebellion, see page 12.

After Simeon died, William Rufus left the position of abbot vacant.

The appointment of a Norman abbot and the rebuilding of the church was part of the Norman reform of the Church.

For more on the Norman Church reform, see pages 27–30.

Now try this

Look at page 27 for more information on Norman Church Reform to help you answer this question.

Give **two** examples of how Ely Cathedral reflects Norman Church reform.

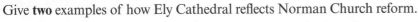

📍 Site investigation **Sample site: Wharram Percy 1**

Have a look at the seven key aspects on page 35. This page and the next give you examples of each aspect for one sample site, as well as examples of change and continuity.

Watch out: you will not be considering Wharram Percy in your exam, so you don't need to learn these facts. You will need to make notes on the seven aspects for **your** selected site.

Context

Wharram Percy is a deserted medieval village. Archaeologists have spent many years finding out about the site. The remains of the medieval church are still there, along with the foundations of two manor houses, 40 peasant houses and various outbuildings. The manor houses and church were the only stone buildings – the rest were built from wood.

The village of Wharram became Wharram Percy after it was given to the Percy family who were Norman.

Change The village was deserted in the early 16th century after the residents were evicted to make room for sheep pasture.

Remains of the church and buildings at Wharram Percy.

1 Location

Wharram Percy is located in a valley in North Yorkshire. People had lived there since prehistoric times, and one of the main roads to the village dates from the Roman period. However, the village was probably founded in the Anglo-Saxon period, between 850 and 950. It grew significantly between the 10th and 12th centuries.

2 Function

Wharram Percy was a rural village. Its functions were:

• to provide accommodation – the lord's manor house and 40 peasants' houses

• to provide a base for people to work the land – sheep, cow, pig and hen bones found at the site show animals were being farmed, and the remains of horses and oxen suggest that these were used to pull ploughs to cultivate the fields.

3 Structure

Change There are two manor houses because in around 1254 the Percy family built themselves a new house – this means that in Norman times the larger manor house at the top of the map would not have existed.

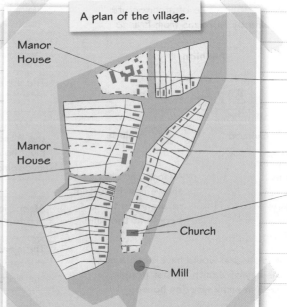

A plan of the village.

Manor House

Made of stone

Manor House

Made of stone

Timber-built

Made of stone

Peasant houses and barns/outhouses for storing grain, hay, animals

Church

Mill

Now try this

What does a site like Wharram Percy tell us about life in a Norman village? Give **three** examples.

📍Site
investigation **Sample site:
Wharram Percy 2**

Make sure you have revised pages 35 and 38 before looking at this page.

4 People

> See page 1 for more on the Danelaw.

Before 1066: The Domesday Book tells us that before 1066, the two main landowners were Lagmann and Carli. A third man, Ketilbjorn, held a smaller portion of land.

Causation The men's names suggest that they had Viking ancestry – this is because Yorkshire had been part of the Danelaw.

1086: William I had confiscated Wharram and given Lagmann and Carli's land to Osbert the Sheriff, and Ketilbjorn's land to a Norman baron, William de Percy.

1254: The Percy family later bought the rest of the village from Osbert's family and the village became known as Wharram Percy.

The earthworks tell us that there were various types of peasant house, dating from before 1066:
- some larger houses, probably owned by freemen
- a row of regular houses and plots with strips of land alongside, probably villeins' houses
- a row of smaller, less regular plots, probably occupied by cottars.

5 Design

The village was dominated by the original manor house and the church. These were the two biggest buildings and show the central importance of the lord and the Church in people's lives.

Change Mills were expensive to build and run, and peasants were charged to use them. The Wharram Percy mill was positioned centrally in the village, showing its importance.

The church was built by the road to impress people passing through the village. The village is linear, with houses following the course of the roads.

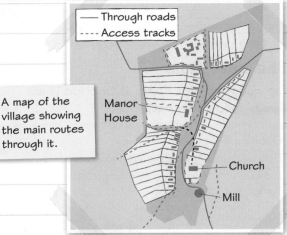

A map of the village showing the main routes through it.

— Through roads
--- Access tracks

Manor House
Church
Mill

6 Culture, values and fashions

Change There are big social changes that we **cannot** see from the site, for example, higher rents meaning that freemen had to become villeins, or the impact of the language barrier when the lord spoke French instead of English.

The different types of housing reflect the social order at the time.

Culture

Wharram Percy

Values

The church was a key feature of the village, reflecting the importance of religion in the period.

The mill was built by the Norman landlord as a sign of prestige.

7 Important events and developments

Change Ownership of the land was transferred to a Norman baron after the Norman Conquest.

Continuity Although the Norman barons developed the village, for most of the inhabitants, day-to-day life would have changed very little.

Change Unlike many other villages in North Yorkshire, Wharram Percy was not affected by William I's 'Harrying of the North'. This indicates that there was little rebellion against Norman rule in the area and inhabitants were willing to accept the change.

Now try this

> You will also need to refer to page 38 to answer this question.

Give **two** facts about Wharram Percy that support the argument that very little changed in village life for peasants after the Conquest.

Exam overview

This page introduces you to the main features and requirements of the Paper 2 Section B exam paper for Norman England, c1066–c1100.

About Paper 2

- Paper 2 is for both your thematic study and your British depth study.
- Section B of the paper covers your British depth study. Norman England, c1066–c1100 is one of the depth study options and includes the historic environment.
- Section B will include questions about other British depth study options. You should **only** answer the questions about Norman England, c1066–c1100.
- You will receive two documents: a question paper, which will contain the questions and interpretations, and an answer booklet.

> The Paper 2 exam lasts for 1 hour 45 minutes (105 minutes). There are 84 marks available in total: 40 marks, plus 4 marks for spelling, punctuation and grammar, for Section A and **40 marks for Section B**. You should spend approximately 50 minutes on Section A and **50 minutes on Section B**, leaving 5 minutes to check your answers.

> The following pages focus on Section B and your British depth study. However, the same exam paper will also include Section A, where you will answer questions on your thematic study.

The questions

> You can see examples of all four questions on pages 41–47 and in the practice questions on pages 48–58.

The questions for Paper 2 Section B will always follow this pattern:

Question 5
How convincing is **Interpretation A** about … ?
Explain your answer using Interpretation A and your contextual knowledge.   **(8 marks)**

> Question 5 targets AO4. AO4 is about **analysing**, **evaluating** and making **substantiated judgements**. Spend about 10 minutes on this question, which is about **analysing and evaluating an interpretation**.

Question 6
Explain what was important about …   **(8 marks)**

> Question 6 targets both AO1 and AO2. AO1 is about showing your **knowledge** and **understanding** of the key features and characteristics of the topic. AO2 is about **explaining** and **analysing** historical events using second order concepts such as causation, consequence, change, continuity, similarity and difference. Spend about 10 minutes on this question, which focuses on **explaining why** an issue or event was important.

Question 7
Write an account …   **(8 marks)**

> Question 7 also targets AO1 and AO2. Spend about 10 minutes on this question, which requires you to write a **narrative account**.

Question 8
[Statement]
How far does a study of [historic environment site] support this statement?
Explain your answer.
You should refer to [historic environment site] and your contextual knowledge.   **(16 marks)**

> Question 8 also targets AO1 and AO2. Spend about 20 minutes on this question, which requires you to make a **judgement** in an extended response about the historic environment site you have studied.

Interpretation skills

Question 5 on your exam paper will ask you to analyse, evaluate and make judgements about interpretations.

What is an interpretation?

For the first question in Section B on the exam paper you will be asked to study an **interpretation** and comment on how convincing it is.

Interpretations are compiled after the time period or event they describe. An interpretation can be text, such as:

- ✓ an account written by a historian
- ✓ a poem
- ✓ a work of fiction.

It might also be an image, such as:

- ✓ a reconstructive drawing
- ✓ a diagram
- ✓ a poster
- ✓ an advertisement
- ✓ a painting.

All interpretations will contain people's views and opinions.

Analysing interpretations

When analysing interpretations, you need to try and work out the **message** of the interpretation. You then need to evaluate the interpretation for Question 5 on your exam paper, which asks you **how convincing** the interpretation is.

Convincing means historically convincing. You need to compare the interpretation to your own knowledge of the period. Does it fit with what you know? If you were to go to Norman England, how close is it to what you would see?

Contextual knowledge

Question 5 will ask you to explain your answer using the interpretation and your **contextual knowledge**. This means that you need to think about what you know about the event or development. Does your knowledge support or contradict the message of the interpretation? Only use knowledge that's relevant to the topic in the question and is linked to what is discussed or shown in the interpretation itself.

Provenance

Before the interpretation in the exam paper you will be given several lines of **provenance** (authorship). This is likely to include some details about the author and their work or experiences, and when their work was published.

You should use the information in the provenance to help you establish the **purpose** of the interpretation. However, you do not need to evaluate the provenance itself in the exam.

Hints and tips for analysing and evaluating interpretations

What's the focus?	What is shown/described?
Interpretations can approach a topic from very specific angles. Sometimes, historians set out to look at one particular aspect, whereas others may want to look at related issues in a broader sense. An artist might want to convey a sense of drama rather than focus on accuracy.	A useful mnemonic here is **PEA**: • **People**: Who is shown/described in the interpretation? Is the picture or description convincing? Why or why not? • **Environment**: Where is the interpretation set? Is it accurate? Why or why not? • **Activity**: What is happening in the interpretation? Is it an accurate representation? Was this a normal occurrence or not?

Remember, you do not need to discuss what is **not** shown. You will only get credit for discussing what **is** shown.

41

Interpretation A

This interpretation is referred to in the worked example on page 43.

SECTION B

Norman England, c1066–c1100

Use **Interpretation A** to answer question 5 on page 43.

Interpretation A   This is an interpretation of the Battle of Hastings in 1066. This engraving is a copy of a painting by Philip James de Loutherbourg. The engraving was made for a history book published in 1804.

You will be given some information about the subject of the interpretation. In this case, you are told that the interpretation shows the Battle of Hastings in 1066.

You will be given short details on where the interpretation comes from. In this case, you are told the type of book and when it was published.

Annotate the interpretation with your ideas. If the interpretation is an image, like this one, think about the details you can see. If the interpretation is a text extract, underline or highlight any important words or phrases and annotate them.

Question 5: Evaluating interpretations

Question 5 on your exam paper will ask you to evaluate how convincing an interpretation is in relation to a particular aspect of the topic. There are 8 marks available for this question.

Worked example

How convincing is **Interpretation A** on page 42 as a depiction of the Battle of Hastings?

Explain your answer using **Interpretation A** and your contextual knowledge.   **(8 marks)**

Sample answer

This picture comes from a nineteenth-century history book, so it wasn't made by someone with first-hand knowledge of the Battle of Hastings.

However, many features of the picture are accurate. It shows the Normans fighting on horseback and the English on foot. It shows the English carrying lances and axes and the Normans using swords. On the other hand, it does not show the Norman archers.

Do not write about what is **not** shown. You will only get credit for discussing what **is** shown.

Start with a clear introduction, stating whether or not you think the interpretation is convincing.

Improved answer

Interpretation A is quite convincing because it includes several important features of the Norman and Anglo-Saxon armies. The Normans are shown on horseback, while the English are shown fighting on foot. This is convincing because we know that the Normans used cavalry and the English didn't. The picture also shows other key differences in armour and weaponry, such as the Normans' armour and swords, and the English fighting with lances and axes. This is an accurate depiction of the differences between the weapons used by the two armies.

The setting of the picture is less convincing as it shows the battle being fought on level ground – we know that the Saxon army stationed themselves on a hill and the Normans had to fight uphill.

The fighting in the picture is also convincing – in medieval battles, people fought hand to hand and battle was brutal. We can see this in the details such as the number of dead on the battlefield – we know that thousands of men were killed – and the English soldiers trying to pull a Norman off his horse.

🔗 **Links**   You can revise the Battle of Hastings on pages 6–8.

The student is correct but remember that you do not need to evaluate the provenance of the interpretation. You only need to evaluate the actual interpretation. These are good details, but the student needs to use their **contextual knowledge** to explain why the details are convincing.

Evaluating an interpretation

- ✓ Consider **how convincing** (believable) the image or text is – is it a good interpretation of what actually happened or what the event would have been like?
- ✓ Think about whether it matches your **contextual knowledge** – what you know about the topic.
- ✓ Comment on **more than one aspect** (part) of the interpretation and link it up with your own knowledge.
- ✓ **Explain** your ideas by giving reasons for the points you make.
- ✓ Finish with a **conclusion** summarising how convincing the interpretation is.

Remember **PEA**! Start with the **people**. Your answer should point out the detail and then link it to your specific knowledge of the period.

Move onto the **environment** – again, focus on a detail and explain why it is/is not convincing by contrasting it with your contextual knowledge.

Then look at the **activity** – describe what is happening in the picture and why it is or isn't convincing.

43

Question 6: Explaining importance

Question 6 on your exam paper is about explaining importance and the significance of an event by referring to its consequences. There are 8 marks available for this question.

Worked example

Explain what was important about Lanfranc's reforms of the English Church in Norman England.

(8 marks)

🔗 **Links** Look at pages 26–30 to revise the changes the Normans made to the English Church.

Sample answer

Lanfranc introduced a new Church hierarchy, with new roles. This was important because it centralised the Church and made it more like the Church in the rest of Europe.

He also introduced synods, a sort of Church council. Bishops all had to hold synods and this allowed Lanfranc to spread reform through the Church more easily and tackle things like Church abuses.

This is a good start, as it covers two consequences of Lanfranc's reforms and it begins to explain why they were important. However, the student needs to include more detailed explanation – for example, why was it important to centralise the Church?

How to explain importance

To answer this question, you need to say **how or why** something was **important**. You should:

☑ refer to two or more **consequences** of the issue or event given in the question – here, the Norman reforms of the English Church

☑ use your **own knowledge** of the period

☑ give **evidence and examples** to support and justify the points you make

☑ use second order concepts in your explanation – a good way to do this is to use sentence starters like 'One reason for this was ...' or 'This was important because ...'.

Improved answer

Lanfranc's reforms of the English Church were important because they brought the Church under control and made it more like the Church elsewhere in Europe.

Lanfranc introduced a new Church hierarchy, including new roles such as archdeacons, who covered similar areas to the shires, and deans, who covered similar areas to the hundreds. This was key because it gave bishops much stronger control over their bishoprics.

This control was strengthened further by the introduction of synods. Synods were Church councils and bishops were expected to hold them to spread the messages of reform. This was important because it gave Lanfranc the ability to push through his reforms.

William and Lanfranc had been horrified at the corruption in the English Church, so a key reform was the ending of abuses like pluralism, simony and nepotism.

Another key factor was the expansion of the role of the parish priest. The number of parish churches doubled between 1066 and 1076, so more people had access to a church and more villages were overseen by a priest. This gave the Church more influence. As well as new churches, most Anglo-Saxon churches were rebuilt in stone, making people more aware of the power of the Church.

Start by signposting your answer and highlighting the points that will be covered.

This paragraph expands on one of the consequences (the new church hierarchy) and the student is using their **knowledge of the period** to give examples and to explain why this change was important (i.e. the bishops had more control).

Link your paragraphs together. Here, the student builds on the previous paragraph, again giving an example and explaining why it was important.

You need to give **at least two** consequences, so this paragraph explores some further examples.

Question 7: Narrative account

Question 7 on your exam paper requires you to write a narrative account analysing how and why a historical event happened. There are 8 marks available for this question.

Worked example

Write an account of the ways in which life in towns changed under the Normans.   **(8 marks)**

Sample answer

There were very few towns in Anglo-Saxon England, and they occurred mostly along the south and east coasts. The Normans built new towns and many existing towns grew under Norman rule. However, other towns, especially where there had been rebellions, suffered. The population of York, for example, fell after 1066.

Life in towns changed under Norman control – the castles that were built caused poverty and the Normans took over the markets.

This answer contains good subject knowledge but is really only narrative. A better answer would explore not only the changes but how they related to the broader **historical context**. For example, why did towns grow?

 Links Look at page 22 to revise life in Norman towns.

What is a narrative account?

A **narrative account** is not simply a description of what happened. To write a successful narrative account you need to:

- ✓ think about **key elements** of the event and how they were **connected**
- ✓ consider what the account needs to do – you may need to think about cause, change, continuity and/or consequence here
- ✓ use your own knowledge of the period
- ✓ structure your narrative logically, so it has a clear order.

Here, the student needs to go on to explain **how** the castles caused poverty, and the impact of Norman control of the markets.

Improved answer

There were very few towns in Anglo-Saxon England. Most were along the south and east coasts because they played a vital part in England's wool trade with Europe. The Normans were keen to exploit the wealth of these towns, and under Norman rule the wool trade – especially with France – expanded. This meant that many towns became larger and more prosperous, as people from the countryside came to the town in search of work and a better life.

Although many towns grew, some did not, especially northern towns like York, which had rebelled against William and had been 'harried' as punishment. Other towns like Norwich, Stafford and Oxford were badly affected by the Norman Conquest, and particularly by castle building, which often involved the demolition of houses and workshops. This affected the prosperity of the towns, meaning that people left them to look for work elsewhere. The Domesday Book tells us that 40 per cent of the houses in Stafford were empty in 1086.

Even towns that did grow felt negative effects. The Normans took control of the lucrative markets, increasing rents and tolls. These changes caused real hardship and increased tensions between the English and the Normans.

Make sure you set your knowledge in the **historical context** – for example, here, the student uses their knowledge to explain that towns grew because the Normans developed the wool trade.

If there were exceptions, you can say why things were different – in this case, for example, because York had rebelled.

Make sure you explain the **effect** of the changes, and not just the changes. Here, the student successfully explains how the building of castles affected the prosperity of towns and how this led to people moving away.

Question 8: Historic environment 1

On your exam paper, the last question for Section B on your British depth study of Norman England will focus on the historic environment. You will be given a statement and asked **how far** a study of your historical site supports the statement. There are 16 marks available for this question.

Worked example

'The main reason for cathedral building under the Normans was to demonstrate their power.'
How far does a study of Ely Cathedral support this statement?
Explain your answer.
You should refer to Ely Cathedral and your contextual knowledge.

(16 marks)

Watch out: You will not be considering Ely Cathedral in your exam. You will need to answer a similar question based on the site **you** have studied.

Remember the **seven key aspects**: location; function; structure; people; design; culture, values and fashions; and important events and developments. Use these aspects to help structure your answer.

You can compare this answer with an improved version on page 47.

🔗 **Links** See pages 36 and 37 for more about Ely Cathedral.

'How far ...' questions

This extended answer question is asking you to balance **evidence** to come up with an argument – a **line of reasoning**. You need to:

✓ describe **aspects**/features of the historical site that support the statement in the question, giving reasons to explain **why** they support the statement

✓ do the same for any aspects/features of the site that either contradict the statement, or that you would expect to see in a typical site but are missing from this one

✓ develop a **sustained** line of reasoning – 'sustained' means you need to present a clear, logical argument **throughout your answer**

✓ use **evidence** from your **site study** and from the **wider historical context**

✓ make a **judgement** – you need to decide 'how far' by reaching a conclusion based on the facts and reasoning in your answer.

Sample extract

Ely had been the centre of Hereward the Wake's rebellion against William. William responded by demonstrating his power over the monastery. Later, the English abbot was replaced by Simeon, a relative of William I. Simeon went on to oversee the rebuilding of the abbey church. This was part of a larger pattern of Norman churchmen replacing English ones.

The Norman programme of church building was a key part of their reform of the English Church. At the same time, the Normans reformed Church practice and ended abuses such as simony. They were partly intended to show that Norman rule was supported by God. At Ely, the Anglo-Saxon building was replaced by a church in the Romanesque style introduced by the Normans.

There were other reasons for church building – William appears to have been a genuinely religious man, and Normandy was famous for its beautiful churches. Building fine new church buildings was also an expression of piety and a desire to glorify God.

 In a full answer, you should begin with a short introduction to signpost your argument.

 Use **evidence** from your **site study** to support your points – here, the student needs to show **how** William demonstrated his power.

 Refer to the **wider historical context**: the events going on in the background.

 Make sure that all your points are **relevant** – this information about church reform is accurate, but not relevant.

 Give a clear answer to the 'how far' part of the question – this is missing here.

Question 8: Historic environment 2

This page contains an improved version of the answer extract given on page 46.

Improved extract

In many ways, Ely cathedral demonstrates the importance of power and prestige to the Normans: it is a splendid building, and must have been a very impressive symbol of the Norman conquest. However, there were other factors behind the building of the cathedrals.

Ely had been the centre of Hereward the Wake's rebellion against William. The rebellion ended in 1070, and although Thurstan, the Anglo-Saxon abbot, was allowed to keep his position, the abbey was punished with a huge fine, and a castle was built close to the abbey – this was a clear symbol of Norman control. When Thurstan died, he was replaced by Simeon, a relative of William I. Simeon went on to oversee the rebuilding of the abbey church. This was part of a larger pattern of Norman churchmen replacing English ones.

The Norman programme of church building was a key part of their reform of the English Church, and it is certainly true that these imposing structures would have been powerful reminders of Norman dominance. They were partly intended to show that Norman rule was supported by God. At Ely, the Anglo-Saxon building was replaced by a church in the Romanesque style the Normans preferred – examples of Romanesque features include the thick walls, the symmetrical construction and the tiers of rounded arches in the nave.

However, it would be a mistake to think that churches were built purely as a symbol of Norman dominance. The building of the cathedrals was part of a wider context of reform – at Ely, the monastic buildings were also rebuilt, reflecting the Norman revival of monasticism. William appears to have been a genuinely religious man, and Normandy was famous for its beautiful churches. Building fine new church buildings was also an expression of piety and a desire to glorify God. More specifically to Ely, the monks at Ely were keen to show off their own status and protect their prestige – it wasn't just the king who used cathedral building to make a point.

This is a good **introduction**. It is short, explains the different sections of the answer and shows that the student is considering both sides of the issue.

Wider historical context

The historic environment question asks you to use both your knowledge of the site and your **contextual knowledge**. You will need to consider the question from two angles:

- ☑ Think about what you know about the topic given in the question – is there evidence for this at the site? For example, if your site is a castle, how many of the main features does it have?

- ☑ Think about the main features of the site – how do they link to the historical period? For example, if your site is a cathedral, the presence of a deanery is evidence of the new roles introduced by Lanfranc's reforms.

Use **evidence** from your study to support the **judgement** you make about the statement in the question. Here, the student uses evidence from their knowledge of the **historical context**, and then moves on to give specific **examples from the site**.

Using a word like 'however' signposts that you are moving on to consider the other side of the argument. This shows that you are following a **sustained line of reasoning**.

Make a clear point in every paragraph, and use examples throughout. Relate your answer back to the site as the student does here.

In your full answer, you should end with a **conclusion** summing up your judgement about **how far** the study of a site supports the statement in the question.

Practice

You will need to refer to the interpretation below in your answer to question 5 on page 49.

SECTION B

Norman England, c1066–c1100

Answer **all four questions** on pages 49 to 55.

Use **Interpretation A** to answer question 5 on page 49.

Interpretation A   An extract describing Norman castles from a book on the history of England by the novelist and historian Peter Ackroyd. It was published in 2011.

> The Norman castles were square masses of masonry, with extraordinarily thick walls and tiny windows. They crush the land beneath them. They are indomitable[1]. They exude an air of gloom and even despair. […] The English hated them as the strongholds of their oppressors. Yet they are, in their own fashion, magnificent creations, born out of the will to power and control that the Normans possessed in full measure.

[1]**indomitable:** impossible to defeat

Practice

Put your skills and knowledge into practice with the following question. You will need to refer to Interpretation A on page 48 in your answer.

> You have 1 hour 45 minutes for the **whole** of Paper 2, which means you have about **50 minutes** for Section B. In the exam, remember to leave 5 minutes or so to check your work when you have finished both Sections A and B.

5 How convincing is **Interpretation A** about the impact of castles on Norman England?

Explain your answer using **Interpretation A** and your contextual knowledge.

(8 marks)

> You need to discuss the content of the interpretation in context – you **must** use your own **contextual knowledge** about the role of Norman castles in your answer.

Guided The interpretation is fairly convincing about the impact of castles on Norman England because it describes accurately how the English felt about them

....

....

....

....

> Spend about 10 minutes on this answer.

....

....

> 🔗 **Links** You can revise Norman castles on page 10.

....

....

....

> Pick out **at least two key details** from the interpretation, for example, the description of the castles, the way people's feelings are described. What do they reveal about the effect of Norman castles? Think about why the Normans built castles.

....

....

....

....

> Do these key details agree with your contextual knowledge or contradict it?

....

....

....

....

....

....

Practice

Use this page to continue your answer to question 5.

....

....

....

....

....

....

....

....

....

....

....

....

....

....

....

Remember, you do not need to discuss what is **not** present in the interpretation. Focus on what is there, and comment on **at least two** aspects, explaining whether or not they fit with your knowledge.

Finish your answer with a clear **conclusion** – it need not be long – setting out how convincing the interpretation is.

Practice

Put your skills and knowledge into practice with the following question.

6 Explain what was important about the feudal system in Norman England.

(8 marks)

This question is asking you to say **how or why** something is **important**.

Guided   Anglo-Saxon society was based on a hierarchy but William developed this system by introducing the feudal system

Spend about 10 minutes on this answer.

Remember, this question asks you to look at the feudal system and the consequences of the changes it caused.

🔗 **Links** You can revise the feudal system on page 15.

You need to think about the Anglo-Saxon system and what the Normans changed. Who was affected by these changes? How were they affected?

How did the feudal system increase William's control? Think about:
• land ownership
• military service
• patronage.
Why were these features of feudalism important?

Practice

Use this page to continue your answer to question 6.

....
....
....
....
....
....
....
....
....
....
....
....
....
....
....

Remember to use your **own knowledge** and back up your points with **evidence** and **examples**.

Practice

Put your skills and knowledge into practice with the following question.

7 Write an account of how William dealt with rebellion between 1066 and 1075.

(8 marks)

Guided There were a number of rebellions against Norman rule between 1066 and 1075. William used a number of strategies to deal with these rebellions. The first local risings began in 1067, such as

....

....

....

....

....

....

....

....

....

....

....

....

....

....

....

....

....

....

Remember that this question asks you to write a narrative account – you need to explain why or how something happened. You will need a clear **structure** to your answer, and you must back up your argument with **evidence** from **your knowledge** of the Norman period.

Spend about 10 minutes on this answer.

Links You can revise the rebellions against Norman rule on pages 11–14.

Think about the **key elements** of the various rebellions and how they are connected – what happened? Who was involved? What did William do? Was his response the same each time?

What were the **causes** of the rebellions? Were they the same each time?

What were the **consequences** of the rebellions? Think about:
• the impact on William's authority
• the involvement of foreign rulers, such as the Danes.

Practice

Use this page to continue your answer to question 7.

....

....

....

....

....

....

....

....

....

....

....

....

....

....

....

How did William's response change? What was the impact of the Harrying of the North and the Siege of Ely?

Remember to signpost your argument with phrases like 'the result of this was ...' and 'this was because ...' when writing your answer.

Practice

Put your skills and knowledge into practice with one of the following questions.

Watch out: In the exam you **must** answer on the Norman site you have studied. You will **not** be given a choice of question in the exam.

This is a **how far** question, so you need to come up with a balanced response: ideas and evidence about the site that support the statement, as well as points that do not.

Choose **either** the Norman site you have studied **or** one of the sites on pages 36–39.

Answer **one** of the following questions.

Remember that for this question on the historic environment you need to **make a judgement** and present a **sustained line of reasoning**.

8a. 'The main change demonstrated by Norman cathedrals was the growing influence of the crown over religion.'

How far does a study of your chosen site support this statement?

Explain your answer.

You should refer to your chosen site and your contextual knowledge.

(16 marks)

🔗 **Links** If your site is a cathedral, consider this question. You could answer this practice question using the information about Ely Cathedral on pages 36 and 37.

8b. 'Life for most people in villages changed little as a result of the Norman Conquest.'

How far does a study of your chosen site support this statement?

Explain your answer.

You should refer to your chosen site and your contextual knowledge.

(16 marks)

🔗 **Links** If your site is a village, consider this question. You could answer this practice question using the information about Wharram Percy on pages 38 and 39.

8c. 'The main change caused by Norman castles was symbolic, not strategic.'

How far does a study of your chosen site support this statement?

Explain your answer.

You should refer to your chosen site and your contextual knowledge.

(16 marks)

If your site is a castle, consider this question.

8d. 'The main factor in the outcome of a battle is the location of the battlefield.'

How far does a study of your chosen site support this statement?

Explain your answer.

You should refer to your chosen site and your contextual knowledge.

(16 marks)

If your site is a battlefield, consider this question.

Turn over to start your answer.

Practice

Use this page to start your answer to question 8.

....

....

....

....

....

....

....

....

....

....

....

....

....

....

....

....

....

....

....

....

....

....

....

....

....

....

....

....

....

Make sure you **consider all key aspects** of the site: location; function; structure; people; design; culture, values and fashions; important events and developments.

It is a good idea to **signpost your answer** by beginning each paragraph with a clear statement in order to give the reader an idea of how the answer will develop. For example, 'There are many ways that Chepstow castle demonstrates the importance of castles in preventing rebellion …' and 'However, there were other reasons for building castles, such as …' This will make your answer easier to write and will also make it easier to understand.

Don't forget the **historical context**. What else was happening at the time? What effect did this have?

Practice

Use this page to continue your answer to question 8.

....

....

....

....

....

....

....

....

....

....

....

....

....

....

....

....

....

....

....

....

....

....

....

....

....

....

....

....

....

Make sure that you **discuss more than one aspect** of the site in your answer.

Practice

Use this page to continue your answer to question 8.

....

....

....

....

....

....

....

....

....

....

....

....

....

....

....

....

Remember to finish your answer with a clear **conclusion**. Your conclusion should refer to the question and sum up the judgement discussed in your answer. For example, 'A study of Ely Cathedral mainly supports the statement that William I increased his power over the English Church.'

ANSWERS

Where an example answer is given, this is not necessarily the only correct response. In most cases there is a range of responses that can gain full marks.

SUBJECT CONTENT

The Normans: conquest and control

1. Anglo-Saxon England

Answers may vary, but you may include points such as:
- the establishing of the kingdom of England under the successors of Alfred the Great
- the flourishing of the Church in the 10th century
- the high quality art and literature produced in England.

2. The succession crisis, 1066

For example, England was attractive because:
- an efficient administration made the king strong as it gave him more control of the kingdom
- the tax system made the king strong because it increased his wealth.

For example, England was unattractive because the earls had a lot of power and wealth. This made the king weak because they could rebel against him.

3. The claimants to the throne

There is no single correct answer to this question, as both claimants had points in their favour. Check that your answer includes the following points:
- the key features of a medieval king (being related to the previous king, chosen by the previous king, supported by the Witan, experience as a warrior, wealth and power) and how these relate to your chosen claimant
- the issue of promises and last words
- the importance of Harold's oath.

Explain why each of these factors makes your chosen claimant's position stronger.

4. Preparing for battle

For example:
- William had to gain support from his fellow Normans – many of them thought invading England was too risky. Harold did not have to do this, because the English did not need to be persuaded to defend England. This meant that Harold could start preparing sooner.
- William had to build enough ships to transport 7000 men, their horses and equipment across the Channel. Harold needed a smaller navy and could assemble it by demanding ships from across the country. This meant that Harold's navy was ready first.

- William needed to defend his men once they arrived in England – this was not something Harold needed to do. William did this by building pre-fabricated castles to take to England. These castles were important in William's invasion.

5. The Battle of Stamford Bridge

For example:
- Hardrada and Tostig were not in the city of York – this made them easier to attack because they didn't have the city walls to defend them. Also, Harold didn't have to capture the city.
- Harold caught Hardrada and Tostig by surprise – the Vikings did not have time to put on their chain-mail.

6. Before the Battle of Hastings

For example: Harold may have been trying to catch William by surprise, which had been a successful tactic at Stamford Bridge. It didn't work, but if it had it would have given Harold a significant advantage. On the other hand, if he had waited, his troops would have outnumbered William's two to one, which would have given Harold a big advantage. In addition, the most experienced soldiers in Harold's army were his housecarls. Many of them were wounded from fighting at Stamford Bridge and all of them had marched 400 miles in two weeks. Giving them a chance to rest may have increased their effectiveness. Finally, Harold was forced to choose a site for the battle quickly. With more time, he may have found a better site.

7. The Battle of Hastings

One advantage of the Norman foot soldiers could include:
- They included archers and crossbowmen, which provided William with a tactical advantage once the shield wall had thinned out.
- William had been able to increase the size of his army by hiring mercenaries.
- They included heavily armoured warriors who could be effective in combat against the English housecarls.
- The mix of troops gave William more tactical options than the English army had.

One disadvantage of the Norman foot soldiers could include:
- They may not have been trained to fight alongside cavalry, making it more difficult to coordinate troops.
- Some were only lightly armoured, making them weak if caught too close to the English shield wall (e.g. within javelin range).
- Those that were mercenaries needed to be paid and would cause trouble if they weren't.

One advantage of the English fyrd could include:
- Bands within the fyrd would have known each other well, making them more effective as part of the shield wall.

- The fyrd system enabled Harold to gather more men for his army despite losses of men at Gate Fulford and Stamford Bridge.

One disadvantage of the English fyrd could include:
- The fyrd was not well trained.
- The fyrd was not well equipped: most would have had farm implements as weapons, and no armour.

8. Reasons for William's victory

There are several possible answers to this question, such as the mistakes Harold made before the battle, the Normans being better equipped and trained, William's superior tactics, or that William was lucky. Any of these answers is fine, as long as you can explain it and support it with evidence, for example: The most important factor was the Normans' superior tactics, because the use of the tactic of feigned retreat was the turning point of the battle.

9. William establishes control

For example, by:
- taking possession of all the land in England and giving a great deal of it to his followers
- building castles
- putting his key allies in charge of strategic areas like the south and the Welsh border.

10. Castles

For example, any three from:
- they dominated the surrounding area, reminding the English that the Normans were in control
- they were used to keep the local population under surveillance
- they were used to garrison soldiers who kept down rebellion
- they ensured that the Normans controlled strategically important places, and could move freely around the country.

11. Early revolts, 1067–68

For example: William dealt with early rebellions as leniently as he could. At first, he was content to let things blow over whenever possible. When there was a direct challenge to his rule – as in Exeter and the earls' rebellion in 1068 – he punished the ringleaders, but gave the people repeated opportunities to submit to him. If they did, they were pardoned. This may have been because he was trying to avoid triggering further rebellions, and wanted to encourage people to be loyal to him by being merciful.

12. Further rebellion, 1069–75

For example: William's response to rebellion became tougher and less forgiving, and he suppressed revolt mercilessly. This was probably because rebellions kept popping up and William didn't have enough soldiers for them to be everywhere at once. The Danes were also involved in the uprisings and they were a threat to William's throne. He had to deal with this weakness.

13. The Harrying of the North

For example: The north of England had been the site of the most serious rebellions against Norman rule. In addition, Viking invasions had usually centred on York (an old Viking city). The Harrying of the North reduced the population and destroyed farming, ensuring the area couldn't mount another revolt or support a Danish invasion.

14. The Norman dynasty

Various answers are possible.
For example:
The most important method William used to secure England was building castles. This was because:
- they allowed him to move troops around to deal with rebellion
- they allowed him to keep control of strategic areas like towns, roads and rivers
- they were a powerful symbol of domination.

Life under the Normans

15. The feudal system

Differences – for example, two from:
- the number of slaves reduced under Norman rule
- the nobles were allowed less land, so they could not build power bases to challenge the king
- William took more control over the ways in which land could be passed on, such as by controlling who tenants' widows could marry, and charging fees when estates changed hands.

Similarities – for example, two from:
- both systems were hierarchies with the king at the top and the peasants/slaves at the bottom
- both systems involved exchanging land for loyalty and/or service
- the Church was an important landowner in both systems.

16. Military service

For example:
- William needed to be sure that he had the soldiers he required, as he was dealing with the constant threat of rebellion.
- Making the knights' duties more formal meant that they always had to do military service, rather than being called up when needed. This made it easier for William to manage his troops.

17. Changes to government

Possible answers include the following.
Features William kept – for example, three from:
- government by Writ
- the system of shires, hundreds and sheriffs
- the Chancery
- the practice of seeking advice from his leading subjects.

Changes that William made – for example, three from
- changing the system of inheritance so that the eldest son inherited
- introducing feudal incidents to give him more control and income
- new roles, for example, castellans
- replacing the Witan with the Curia Regis
- reducing the power of the nobles.

18. The legal system

For example:
- The Anglo-Saxon legal systems were effective.
- Keeping the existing systems gave continuity and helped to show that he was the legitimate monarch.

19. Trials and punishment

For example: The murdrum fine tells us that relations between the English and the Normans were hostile. The Normans introduced the fine because they were being attacked, or feared they might be, and they thought that the English were hiding the attackers.

20. The Domesday Book

For example: By collecting information about England at the end of Edward the Confessor's reign, and again in 1086, William was able to establish himself as Edward's legitimate heir, and to ensure that all transfers of land were final and could not be questioned.

21. Villages

Changes – for example, three from:
- there were fewer slaves under the Normans
- rents increased
- the lord had a different language and followed different customs
- many buildings, such as churches, were rebuilt
- Forest Law meant that peasants could no longer hunt in the forests.

Continuity – for example, three from:
- the work people did stayed the same
- most people were still tenants who worked for a lord
- people lived in the same houses.

22. Towns

Better – for example, two from:
- many towns became bigger and more prosperous
- the guilds improved trade.

Worse – for example, two from:
- market rents and tolls increased
- castle building meant that houses and workshops were destroyed
- some towns in rebellious areas were attacked.

23. Food

For example: Although they were at risk of shortages if the harvests were bad, the poor probably had a healthier diet. Their diet was quite boring but they ate lots of vegetables and had access to eggs, beans and dairy products. The rich ate very little fresh food, and more of it was sweetened.

24. Work

Advantages – for example, one from:
- a wider range of jobs
- it was possible to climb the hierarchy and make a good living.

Disadvantages – for example, one from:
- most people worked as servants or unskilled labourers
- becoming a craftsman involved several years of hard work for no/low pay.

25. Housing

For example: In most towns, if the population increased, the housing situation would have become worse because there would have been overcrowding. The overcrowding would also have led to increased sanitation problems.

The Norman Church and monasticism

26. The Anglo-Saxon Church

For example, two from:
- The Church was wealthy and had a lot of land. William may have wanted to reduce the amount of land the Church had.
- People were very concerned with going to heaven, which gave the Church a lot of influence. William might have felt that his subjects should pay more heed to him.
- The Anglo-Saxon Church was corrupt and he wanted to change this.

27. Lanfranc and Church reforms

For example, two from:
- William was prepared to agree to reforms that Lanfranc wanted, even if they weakened his own power, because he had promised the Pope he would make reforms and he had chosen Lanfranc to carry them out.
- William genuinely believed that Church reform was the right thing to do.
- Lanfranc needed William's support during the battle for primacy with Thomas of York.

28. Church building

For example, two from:
- Many village churches were rebuilt and those dedicated to English saints were re-dedicated to other saints instead.
- Impressive cathedrals dominated the landscape and were a reminder of Norman power.
- New cathedrals were a way of showing that the Norman Conquest was supported by God.

29. William II and the Church

For example:

- He kept important posts empty so that he could keep the money.
- He wanted to reduce the Pope's influence over the Church so that he had greater control himself.
- He was less pious than William I and the Church thought he had poor morals.

30. Relations with the Papacy

For example:

- The king was able to appoint senior churchmen – this power gave him a lot of patronage.
- Popes often wanted to be able to appoint bishops and archbishops themselves, which led to tension with rulers all Christians were supposed to obey the Pope, which might mean that he could challenge a king's authority.

31. Monastic reform

For example: It gave Lanfranc more control over the monasteries and how they were run, and ensured that all monks and nuns were seen to be pious.

32. New monastic orders

For example, two from:

- The Cluniacs followed the Rule of St Benedict strictly. This was important because monastic standards had fallen during the Anglo-Saxon period.
- Landowners built splendid priories to increase their prestige. This led to the increased spread and status of monasticism in England.
- The Cluniacs had a close relationship with the Papacy, meaning that they helped spread Papal reforms.

33. Monastic life

For example, two from:

- many would not have liked the stricter rules on diet and clothing
- many monasteries had not followed the routine of services
- many did not like the change in the liturgy where English was replaced with Latin.

34. Learning and language

For example: Most English people were peasants and would have continued to speak English. They would have heard Latin in church, which would have been a big change, but the use of Latin as a government language would not have affected most people because they could not read. On the other hand, most peasants would have had a new lord who spoke French and so they would no longer have shared a language with their lord. In towns, French was spoken by the middle classes as well as by the nobility, and French words were absorbed into English, so French probably had the bigger impact.

The historic environment of Norman England

35. Site investigation

Answers will depend on the site you have studied. For example, using the sample site Ely Cathedral on pages 36 and 37:

- Location – The cathedral is in an area of marsh called the Fens. In Norman times, Ely was an island.
- Function – The cathedral was built as the abbey church.
- Structure – The cathedral is built in a cruciform (cross) shape.
- People – The building of the cathedral was overseen by Abbot Simeon, a Norman relative of William I.
- Design – The nave features three rows of rounded arches.
- Culture, values and fashions – The cathedral was built in the Romanesque style favoured by the Normans.
- Important events and developments – Ely was the site of Hereward the Wake's rebellion.

36. Sample site: Ely Cathedral 1

For example, two from:

- a building that dominated the surrounding landscape
- high quality materials, such as stone and marble
- it was one of the largest buildings in northern Europe
- it included Romanesque design using the latest Norman fashions.

37. Sample site: Ely Cathedral 2

For example, two from:

- a Norman abbot was appointed
- the rebuilding adopted the Romanesque style favoured by the Normans
- new monastic buildings reflected the revival of monasticism.

38. Sample site: Wharram Percy 1

For example, three from:

- The Normans rebuilt the church in stone, showing that the village was affected by Norman Church reforms.
- Animal remains tell us about the sort of agriculture in the village – both animals and crops were farmed.
- We can see from the different sizes of peasant houses that there were probably freemen, villeins and cottars in the village.
- We can see that peasants had their own plots as well as farming the main fields.
- We can see that the lord's house and the church were the most important buildings – as they were the only ones built in stone.

39. Sample site: Wharram Percy 2

For example, two from:

- One landowner was replaced by another – the peasants were still peasants.
- The peasants' houses were not rebuilt – they stayed in the same houses.
- The village was still a farming village, so the peasants' day-to-day life would have stayed the same.

PRACTICE
49. Practice

5   For example:
The interpretation is fairly convincing about the impact of castles on Norman England because it describes accurately how the English felt about them. We know that the English did hate the castles built by the Normans, and saw them as a sign of oppression, as it says in the interpretation. Most castles were built on mottes, so that they dominated the landscape. The interpretation also mentions the Norman 'will to power and control'. This is convincing as William was increasingly ruthless in his attempts to bring England under his control and castles were an important method of doing this. He often built castles where there had been rebellions, for example, at Exeter and Ely.
However, the description of the castles themselves is less convincing. The interpretation talks about 'square masses of masonry' with 'thick walls and tiny windows'. The Norman castles that survive today were built of stone, but the vast majority of Norman castles were not like this – they were built from timber and earth so that they could be built quickly. Although some stone castles were built early in William's reign (mostly on the borders with Scotland and Wales), most of the castles like the ones described in the interpretation came later. For example, Canterbury Castle was one of the first castles built by William in 1066 but the wooden motte and bailey was only rebuilt in stone in the reign of Henry I.
Overall, though, the interpretation is convincing as a description of the impact of Norman castles on England.

51. Practice

6   For example:
Anglo-Saxon society was based on a hierarchy but William developed this system by introducing the feudal system. This meant that all of the land in England belonged to the king. The king granted land to barons and bishops, who became his tenants-in-chief. These tenants-in-chief then granted land to their followers. This was important because everyone who wanted to hold land depended on the king's favour. The people who were immediately affected were the Anglo-Saxon earls and thegns, who either lost their land entirely, had to rent land they had once owned, or who had their landholdings reduced. This was important because it meant that

land was concentrated in the hands of people William could trust, and because it reduced the power of the English nobility. Another key feature of feudalism was the formalising of military service. Each tenant-in-chief agreed to provide a certain number of knights. This was similar to the way that Anglo-Saxon thegns fought for the king in return for their land. However, there were some key differences. Knights always had to perform military service – usually at least 40 days – rather than being called upon when needed. This was important because it allowed William to garrison castles and put down rebellions – a key part of gaining control of England. The feudal system gave William enormous powers of patronage and he began to assert more control over his tenants. When a tenant died, he charged a fee, decided whether the tenant's widow could remarry, and controlled the land if there was no heir. This increased his powers of patronage even more. William also introduced new laws called feudal incidents. If a tenant died without an heir, their land was returned to the lord, who could keep it, sell it or grant it to someone else.

53. Practice

7   For example:
There were a number of rebellions against Norman rule between 1066 and 1075. William used a number of strategies to deal with these rebellions. The first local risings began in 1067, such as Eadric's rebellion on the Welsh border and Eustace of Boulogne's attack on Dover. These were fairly minor and were dealt with by William's chosen deputies while he was in Normandy. The first more serious rising was in Exeter. William besieged the city, but when they surrendered, William treated the rebels leniently in return for them swearing loyalty. This lenient approach may have been to avoid triggering further rebellion, or to encourage people to be loyal by being merciful to them.
In 1068, Earls Edwin and Morcar led a rebellion of Anglo-Saxon nobles. They were angry about the loss of their land, taxes and William's castle building. William took his troops north and put down the rebellion. Once again, he treated Edwin and Morcar leniently. However, he decided to put a Norman in charge of the north and appointed Robert de Comines Earl of Northumbria. Robert's men looted Durham, triggering a revolt in which de Comines and his men were killed. This sparked another rising in the north, and Edgar Ætheling and Earl Gospatric joined in. William took his army north again, crushed the rebels and retook York, putting his most trusted friend, William FitzOsbern, in charge. He had given up on trying to include English nobles in his government. From now on, only Normans would be in charge.

In September 1069, the Danes sent a fleet to England and joined forces with the English rebels. Again, they headed for York. At this point, William's response became tougher and less forgiving. He suppressed the revolt mercilessly, laying waste to York. William was having to deal with constant rebellions and he didn't have enough soldiers for them to be everywhere at once. The rebellions were also a threat to his authority. In addition, the Danes were involved in the latest uprising and they were a threat to William's throne. He dealt with this by paying the Danes to leave and then, at the beginning of 1070, he and his men attacked the north of England, tracking down rebels, destroying villages and burning crops and livestock. The result was widespread famine and in 1086, whole areas were described in the Domesday Book as 'waste'. By the time of Hereward's rebellion in Ely, William was not taking any chances – he besieged the town, put down the rebellion, and executed and imprisoned the ringleaders.

55. Practice

8   For example:
Answers to Question 8 should:
• balance evidence to make a clear, logical argument
• describe any aspects/features that support the statement and explain why
• describe any aspects/features that either contradict the statement, or that you would expect but are missing, and explain why
• include the seven key factors (location; function; structure; people; design; culture, values and fashions; and important events and developments)
• relate your knowledge to the site and the site to your knowledge – you need to do both!
• make a judgement about which side of the argument is stronger – this is your 'how far'.
For example, an answer to question 8a. about Norman cathedrals, referring to Ely Cathedral, might look like this:
In many ways, the influence Norman kings had over the Church is evident from a study of Ely Cathedral – for example, English churchmen being replaced by Normans and the replacing of Anglo-Saxon churches with new buildings. However, there are also some signs at Ely that the Church could act independently. Ely Cathedral is an example of the huge church-building programme that the Normans introduced to demonstrate their power and show that the Conquest was supported by God. Apart from Westminster Abbey, every cathedral in England was rebuilt. At the time Ely Cathedral was built, it was the abbey church (it only became a cathedral in 1109). The cathedral was built on a bigger scale than the church it replaced, and it dominated the flat landscape of the

surrounding Fens. Abbot Simeon chose to rebuild the church in the Romanesque style that the Normans had introduced to England. The Romanesque influence can be seen in the thick walls built in high-quality stone, the cruciform (cross-shaped) structure, and the design of the nave which features three rows of the rounded arches that are a key characteristic of Romanesque architecture.
In 1070, Ely had been the centre of the rebellion led by Hereward the Wake. Once the rebellion was over, William demonstrated his power by building a castle close to the abbey church. He also fined the abbey for its involvement in the rebellion. William allowed Thurstan – the Anglo-Saxon abbot – to keep his post, but as soon as Thurstan died, Simeon (a relative of William's) was appointed instead. After that, all the abbots (and later bishops) of Ely were Norman. This is an example of how the Norman kings influenced the Church by replacing English churchmen with Normans. Another feature of Norman Church reform was the revival of monasticism. The building of the cathedral was financed by the Benedictine monastery. However, the Normans also replaced the monastic buildings (although they were later replaced themselves and haven't survived). This is another sign of the growing Norman influence over the Church.
However, there are also some signs that the Church could assert its independence from the crown. The first is that the abbey participated in Hereward's rebellion in 1070, although William later punished them for it. As well as the fine he imposed, he took lots of the abbey lands and gave them away to his followers. Abbot Simeon and his successor managed to get most of them back. Under William Rufus, there was more conflict between the Church and the crown – Archbishop Anselm openly criticised the king and complained about him leaving posts empty so that he could keep the revenue. Ely is an example of this – William Rufus did not appoint a replacement when Simeon died. Anselm also wanted to reform the Church in ways that William Rufus did not like.
When Henry I took the throne in 1100, he agreed to some of Anselm's demands, including appointing a new Abbot of Ely, Richard de Clare. During the Investiture Crisis, Richard initially supported Anselm before backing down and swearing allegiance to the king.
Overall, the Norman kings did increase their influence over the Church and although there were periods of conflict – especially under William Rufus – in general, the king maintained control. At Ely, key features of this reform and influence can be seen – e.g. the church-building programme and the replacement of English churchmen with Normans – so a study of Ely Cathedral does support the statement.